D1617344

Science in the Subarctic

SCIENCE IN THE SUBARCTIC

Trappers, Traders, and the Smithsonian Institution

Debra Lindsay

Foreword by William W. Fitzhugh

Smithsonian Institution Press
Washington and London

Editor: Rosemary Sheffield
Designer: Janice Wheeler

Printed in the United States of America

01 00 99 98 87 96 95 94 93
10 9 8 7 6 5 4 3 2 1

Library of Congress Cataloging-in-Publication Data

Lindsay, Debra.
Science in the Subarctic : trappers, traders, and the Smithsonian Institution / by
Debra Lindsay.
p.   cm.
Includes bibliographical references and index.
ISBN 1-56098-233-0
1. Research—Arctic regions—History—19th century. 2. Natural history—Arctic
regions—19th century. 3. Smithsonian Institution—History—19th century.
4. North America—Description and travel—1851–1880. 5. Scientists—North
America. 6. Naturalists—North America. I. Title.
Q180.A6L56   1993
508.92—dc20   92-29811

British Library Cataloging-in-Publication Data available

Cover: Robert Kennicott after his return from the north. Smithsonian Institution
photo 43604

♾ The paper used in this publication meets the minimum requirements of the
American National Standard for Permanence of Paper for Printed Library Materials Z39.48-1984.

TO MY FAMILY

CONTENTS

CONTENTS

FOREWORD

In 1859, when the Smithsonian's assistant secretary, Spencer Fullerton Baird, sent a young naturalist named Robert Kennicott into
the wilds of northwestern Canada to make collections for the
embryonic Institution, Baird could not have imagined the long-
term consequences of that opportunistic act. Baird had already
cleared the way by contacts with Hudson's Bay Company senior
authorities and had arranged for field support from the company.
The expedition was to be the first major test of Baird's method of
field science in a remote region of North America. A naturalist's
paradise inhabited by unacculturated native peoples, the region
was full of game and Baird's favorite scientific subjects—birds,
nests, and eggs. Kennicott, a brilliant field collector and budding
scientist, was the perfect man for the job. Already skilled in wilderness survival and interested in oology and ornithology, he could be
expected to have great success. What neither Baird nor Kennicott
anticipated was that the venture would become the foundation for
a long tradition of Smithsonian collecting and scientific studies in
the Arctic and the subarctic.

The pioneering nature of that effort is quite obvious to us today.
Kennicott's collection was the first large systematic natural history
collection to be made in northwestern North America, and it

served as a model for future field science projects at the Smithsonian and elsewhere. It also provided a practical test of the field method Baird had devised for use throughout the Americas. The result was the collection of several thousand animals, plants, and ethnographic specimens from a completely unknown—and largely unexplored—part of the continent, just barely opened to agents of the Hudson's Bay Company and frontier traders and explorers. In addition to the superb array of natural history material that Kennicott acquired, his artifacts from native Athapaskan and Inuit peoples were destined to become the largest and most important ethnographic collections in existence from those groups.

Baird's field collecting method emphasized the collection of large numbers of carefully documented "voucher" specimens from a given region; such specimens, with later description and analysis, established a firm empirical basis for scientific classification. With analysis of field documentation and careful comparison of specimens, the method supported classification studies that, at higher levels of abstraction, revealed geographic, evolutionary, and historical relationships. The method applied equally to species of animals and plants, to languages, and to ethnographic studies. As the study region was gradually expanded, larger patterns developed that provided solutions to major problems of biological and cultural classification. Baird was particularly aware of the pristine conditions for collecting in northwestern Canada, the Northwest Coast, and Russian America. The prospects of expanding such analyses toward the Northwest, into Alaska, and eventually across Bering Strait into Asia were the larger vision that inspired Baird's labors as a research organizer in northwestern North America. Kennicott's later Alaskan work as leader of the Western Union Telegraph survey became the Smithsonian's entrée into Russian America, influenced the purchase of Alaska, and resulted in the training of the first generation of America's Alaskan scientists, including William Healey Dall, Henry Wood Elliott, and others.

In addition to making great contributions to field collecting, the Baird-Kennicott work in the Mackenzie region established the science plan for the Smithsonian's later collecting programs in Alaska and Ungava. In most cases the collecting program was organized by Baird, who appointed a naturalist to take up residence in the field, make carefully documented collections, and organize collecting efforts by local post managers and native assistants. The Smithsonian provided collecting equipment, guns, and trade goods and paid for the services of native collectors by credits at the Hudson Bay Company posts. Often Baird succeeded in placing his naturalists in the employ of other government agencies that paid their salaries while in their spare time they collected for the Smithsonian, or he made similar arrangements with local people.

One of the most important innovations of Kennicott's Mackenzie program was the involvement of native collectors. Roderick MacFarlane, a Hudson's Bay Company agent, used native people extensively and to great advantage, making important collections of animals, birds, and ethnographic objects during the winter season when post managers and most naturalists were not out and about. The use of native collectors also provided other advantages, including the acquisition of native names, terminology, and observations on animal behavior, on biological phase changes, and on ethnographic data.

As Lindsay notes, the northern field collecting method of Baird and Kennicott relied on organizational efforts as well as scientific skill and training. Kennicott's successful recruitment of Hudson's Bay Company factors was based on Baird's political and financial backing and a system of overt and covert rewards. Similar techniques were employed in later Smithsonian collecting programs in Alaska and Canada. Lindsay correctly points out the central role that the Hudson's Bay Company factors and native peoples played in that process. Although that role is clearly evident in the collection documentation and was acknowledged in the Smithsonian annual reports of the day, it is not widely known today.

Little has been written about the history of early scientific work in the north, and still less about the history of Smithsonian northern science. While scientists have proceeded with new field studies, historians have tended to emphasize exploration. Arctic historians have rarely considered the role of scientific work specifically and of scientific institutions in general. In this pioneering work Debra Lindsay provides us with a fascinating early chapter in the conduct of northern science as practiced by one of the leading scientific institutions of the day. Her work should be a stimulus and a challenge for a new approach to arctic and subarctic history, one that delves behind the specimens themselves and into the methods, motivations, characters, and personal relationships of the early collectors.

WILLIAM W. FITZHUGH

Arctic Studies Center
National Museum of Natural History
Smithsonian Institution

PREFACE AND
ACKNOWLEDGMENTS

Studies in the history of science are often devoted to the discoveries
and contributions of great theorists. The focus here, however, is on
the work of one of North America's lesser-known nineteenth-
century natural scientists, on the fieldwork of a little-known field
naturalist, and on the work of a group of virtually unknown collectors who donated an unprecedented number of northern natural
history specimens to a scientific institution. The scientist is Spencer
Fullerton Baird, the first assistant secretary in charge of natural
history at the Smithsonian Institution; Robert Kennicott is the
young naturalist who went into the far north on Baird's behalf;
and Hudson's Bay Company fur traders and northern native peoples are the collectors upon whom Baird depended for his northern
natural history specimens. Between 1859 and 1869, these men and
women submitted more than 12,000 zoological and anthropological specimens to the Smithsonian Institution.

Baird was one of his generation's foremost authorities on
ornithology, herpetology, and ichthyology; his objective as assistant
secretary was nothing less than establishing the Smithsonian Institution as the preeminent repository for North American natural
history collections. In his 37 years at the Smithsonian, first as
assistant secretary and then as secretary, Baird went a long way

toward realizing his goal. Even during the 1870s the museum and the Natural History Department were important components of contemporary perceptions of the Smithsonian as the symbol of science in America. Although it had been established only in 1846, the Institution was already imbued with an "aura of antiquity."[1] Much of its early reputation rested on Baird's work as collector, administrator, and scientist.

Baird's role in nineteenth-century North American science extended beyond the curatorial and the bureaucratic, however. The assistant secretary was instrumental in bringing about the systematization and rationalization of field methods that occurred in the natural sciences at midcentury. Many of his procedural dicta were eventually adopted by his contemporaries, especially the ornithologists. But the northern traders and native collectors who collected specimens for the Smithsonian, and who were recruited and trained by Robert Kennicott in conformity with Baird's early instructions, were some of the first fieldworkers to apply the Bairdian approach. Part 1 of *Science in the Subarctic* is therefore devoted to an examination of Baird's research goals, as well as to the strategies Baird developed to realize those goals. Analyses of Baird's reasons for wanting to direct and control fieldwork, as well as descriptions of the preliminary steps that were taken to ensure that fieldwork conformed with Smithsonian standards, cast new light on his role at the Smithsonian and in North American science and establish a context for the detailed examination of northern fieldwork found in Part 2. Kennicott's eagerness to return north just three years after arriving home from an initial northern expedition is also understandable, given Baird's priorities and programs. Kennicott set out for Russian America in the spring of 1865 to complete the field studies he had begun in 1859 in the Mackenzie River District of the Hudson's Bay Company's northern territories.

In addition to examining the scientific processes and products of Smithsonian-sponsored fieldwork, Part 2 contains detailed descriptions of nineteenth-century life. In some ways, the information about life at the Hudson's Bay Company's northern posts merely extends work already done by fur trade social historians, but knowledge of the daily routines, recreational pastimes, and interpersonal relationships of traders is also essential for understanding how science functioned within the lives of northern collectors. Indeed, an intimate knowledge of their culture is necessary even to recognize the factors that motivated traders and trappers to volunteer their services in aid of science. Scientific activities were but one facet of the social fabric of these collectors' lives; a certain degree of familiarity with northern life allows analyses that go beyond generalizations about the recreational or intellectual appeal of science. Neither tedium nor inquisitiveness alone could have stimulated northerners into becoming the prodigious collectors that they were. Analyses of their scientific work would be incomplete without reference to a larger context.

The Mackenzie River collectors, both native and European, nurtured their relationship with the Smithsonian because it was in their interests to do so. Collectors traded specimens for both economic commodities and extra-economic rewards, and they valued their connection with the scientific community. Although some specimens were no doubt procured outside that system of exchange, for the most part specimens were a commodity. The efforts of the more educated European or Euro-Canadian traders were repaid with books and alcohol, as well as with official recognition in scientific journals and the collegiality of Smithsonian scientists. In addition to such recognition, fieldwork offered these men an opportunity to enhance their prestige and social status. Other collectors, especially the native collectors, were motivated by economics. Native people exchanged their labor and their expertise for American consumer items and for goods from the Hudson's Bay Company stores.

Ostensibly, Kennicott's 1865 Russian American expedition, which was supported by the Western Union Telegraph Company, differed little from the Mackenzie River expedition. But when Kennicott went to the Mackenzie River District in 1859, the Hudson's Bay Company had been supporting science, at least tangentially, for almost two centuries. Although telegraphy was itself a science, Western Union demonstrated in 1865 that it had neither the capacity nor the desire to promote anything other than communications technology. Part 3 describes the trials and tribulations of Kennicott's second trip north, examines Kennicott's uneasy and unprofitable association with the trip's corporate sponsor, and shows how Western Union's expedition differed from the Mackenzie River expedition. Whereas both employees and managers of the Hudson's Bay Company actively supported Kennicott's 1859 collections in the Mackenzie River District, Western Union officials and members of the 1865 expedition supported Kennicott's scientific work only in principle. The corporation made few substantive contributions to Kennicott's work, and the members of the expedition who were hired to build the telegraph hindered, rather than helped, Kennicott's attempts to do nontelegraphic work. Few specimens and little data had been collected by Kennicott's party in Russian America between July 1865, when the scientific corps reached St. Michael's, and the spring of 1867, when the United States government purchased Alaska from the Russians. One of Kennicott's assistants, William Healey Dall, stayed on to make extensive collections, especially of invertebrates, after the expedition left Alaska, but the 1865 expedition was neither a curatorial nor a procedural success.

Science in the Subarctic is ultimately an examination of two episodes in the history of early Smithsonian-sponsored fieldwork. Because this study examines why Smithsonian scientists wanted to direct and control data collecting procedures, as well as how they endeavored to regulate data collection by focusing on field-workers—specifically, the Hudson's Bay Company employees and native peoples living in Arctic America, as well as the individuals attached to the Western Union expedition—two archival collections have been indispensable. This book would have been inconceivable without access to the documents, artifacts, and rare books in the Smithsonian Institution Archives at Washington, D.C., and in the Hudson's Bay Company Archives at the Provincial Archives of Manitoba, and I thank both archives for the privilege of using their collections. More specifically, I would like to thank Smithsonian archivists Bill Deiss and Susan Glenn, whose knowledge of the Hudson's Bay Company collections was invaluable. Similarly, my research benefited from the expertise of Judith Beattie, Debra Moore, Anne Morton, and Shirlee A. Smith, archivists at the Hudson's Bay Company Archives in Winnipeg, Manitoba. John Bovey and Anna ten Cate, archivists at the British Columbia Provincial

Archives, were also most gracious in making available their records on the Western Union Telegraph Company.

Although I alone am responsible for any errors or omissions that might be found within the text, I am at the same time indebted to several people for their help with this book. I would like to thank Jack Bumsted at the University of Manitoba, Jennifer Brown at the University of Winnipeg, Hannah Gay at Simon Fraser University, and Rosemary Sheffield of Austin, Texas, for their comments and suggestions on the manuscript. I also thank Victor Lytwyn of the University of Manitoba for the maps he drew to depict some obscure points. I am also grateful for the guidance and assistance given by several people at the Smithsonian. Peter Cannell, the science acquisitions editor at Smithsonian Institution Press, and William Fitzhugh, from the Department of Anthropology at the National Museum of Natural History, deserve special mention, as does Phil Angle from the Division of Birds (National Museum of Natural History). The Office of Fellowships and Grants at the Smithsonian Institution and St. John's College at the University of Manitoba also have my appreciation. Financial assistance provided by the Office of Fellowships and Grants funded travel to the Smithsonian Archives, and St. John's College provided office space and a congenial atmosphere—first while I was writing the doctoral dissertation upon which this book is based, and later when I was revising my thesis for publication. Finally, I would like to thank my family—Larry, David, Catherine, Sean, and Tyra-Lynn.

INTRODUCTION

In 1850 when Spencer Fullerton Baird received word that he had been chosen assistant secretary in charge of natural history at the Smithsonian Institution, he quickly resigned his post as professor of natural history at Dickinson College in Carlisle, Pennsylvania. He saw great potential in the Smithsonian, both for science and for his own career. The Smithsonian appointment meant that he could be a full-time practicing naturalist, and there was much for Baird and other naturalists to do.

Like most naturalists in the first half of the nineteenth century, Baird was familiar with the many fields of study included within natural history. In addition to having a working knowledge of the scientific literature, Baird had had responsibility for the translation and editing of the *Iconographic Encyclopedia* (1851), an American version of Heck-Brockhaus's *Bilder Atlas zum Konversations Lexikon,* and he had conducted bibliographical research, including preparatory work on the *Bibliographia Zoologiae et Geologiae* (Agassiz, Strickland, and Jardine, 1848–54)—all of which provided him with the scholarly basis for a comprehensive critique of the natural sciences in North America.[1]

Baird pointed out that only a small percentage of the flora and fauna of North America had been examined, described, identified, and classified, despite some impressive studies by both European and North American naturalists. Descriptions of North American natural history were an integral component of travel literature and were appended to the books that chronicled the progress and achievements of Russian, German, French, and English explorations in the New World.[2] Nevertheless, little was known about the natural history of North America. The lists and catalogues that had been compiled by naturalists such as John Lawson, Mark Catesby, George Edwards, John Reinhold Forster, Peter Kalm, and Thomas Pennant also left many gaps.[3]

Those early catalogues were, however, soon joined by others. The first important one of the nineteenth century, was Alexander Wilson's *American Ornithology* (1808–14). Wilson's book was also the first comprehensive study of a single class of North American animals, and it established a foundation for subsequent work by Charles Lucien Bonaparte, John James Audubon, and Thomas Nuttall.[4] Audubon, in conjunction with his sons and John Bachman, produced a catalogue of North American mammals, as did Richard Harlan.[5] The famous American naturalist Thomas Say wrote one book on North American insects and one on the shells of North American mollusks. Another early American naturalist, John Edwards Holbrook, described North American reptiles.[6] Several important botanical studies had also been undertaken, including the work of Berthold Seemann, Heinrich G. Bongard, F. A. Michaux, Nuttall, Amos Eaton, Lewis C. Beck, John Torrey, and Asa Gray.[7] Like the early zoological studies, they were limited, identifying and describing only a small fraction of the plant species found in North America.

One of the most famous zoological treatises was published by the St. Petersburg Academy of Science in 1827: Peter Pallas's *Zoographia Rosso-Asiatica* contained much that was relevant to arctic America. John Richardson's *Fauna Boreali-Americana* (1829–36) and a companion piece, William Hooker's *Flora Boreali-Americana* (1833–40), were the authoritative works on the natural history of North America's northernmost regions, however.[8] But even they were unavoidably incomplete, limited by the routes of the Franklin expeditions and by the quality and quantity of specimens available for examination.[9] Omitted from them were species found in areas not visited by Sir John Franklin and the scientists who accompanied his overland expedition in search of the Northwest Passage, and species living outside the areas visited by the John Ross expedition (1818), the three Parry expeditions (1819–25), the Beechey expedition (1824–25), and the Back expedition (1833–35). Although Richardson had received ornithological and mammalian specimens from Hudson's Bay Company men stationed in the Rocky Mountains, on the Labrador coast, in the Athabasca and Albany river districts, and at Cumberland House, as well as examining privately owned collections, his studies were still incomplete.[10] Species from the Upper Yukon, along the arctic coast, and around Great Slave Lake were not included in *Fauna Boreali-Americana*, and the zoology of Russian America was even less well known.[11] Some natural history specimens had been collected at Sitka, but explorers had concentrated on the acquisition of geographical data when visiting the mainland.[12]

The inadequacies of the zoological and botanical literature reflected the limitations imposed by incomplete data—a limitation Baird proposed to rectify. In his first report to Congress, Baird identified the deficiencies of the North American data base, noting that both public and private natural history collections had many shortcomings.[13] Birds and mollusks had received considerable attention, but collections were still selective. Complete series of eastern birds were available, but few avian specimens had been collected west of the Mississippi River. Similarly, conchology was a popular pursuit, but the bodies contained inside of mollusk shells had been completely ignored. And few collections contained reptiles, amphibians, crustaceans, insects (excluding coleoptera and lepidoptera), fishes, worms, echinoderms, algae, or other marine life. Botanical collections were equally inadequate. Taxonomic revision, as well as description and identification, was hampered by the empirical deficiencies. Monographic studies were impossible without access to greatly increased collections, as were problem-oriented research programs. Specimens had to be collected and preserved before being identified and classified; the resulting data were, in turn, necessary to verify hypotheses regarding the origins of, and relationships among, North American species. As assistant secretary in charge of natural history, Baird viewed the advancement of the North American natural sciences, initially through increased accessions, to be his duty and privilege.

The task Baird set for himself and the Smithsonian was, simplistically stated, gap filling. In essence, however, Baird had to contend with two different problems. Several classes of North American plants and animals had been ignored by the scientific community, and the contents of even the most recent publications were inadvertently selective. That problem was a taxonomic one. Baird also had a practical problem: how to get as many specimens as possible, from as wide a geographical range as possible, as quickly and cheaply as possible. Unless he could improve upon earlier data gathering systems, scientists would not receive the large numbers of high-quality specimens needed for systematics and taxonomy.[14]

Baird approached the accessions problem pragmatically. European scientists had been receiving specimens from the New World via exploring expeditions for more than a century, and during the first half of the nineteenth century, North American scientists, including Baird himself, received specimens and data as a result of explorations in the interior of North America. During the 1850s Baird and Charles Girard, a former assistant to Louis Agassiz, examined and catalogued the reptilian and amphibian specimens that had been collected more than 10 years earlier by the Great United States Exploring (Wilkes) Expedition.[15] Baird and Girard also studied the amphibian and reptilian specimens collected by the Pacific Coast and Mexican Boundary surveys. Identifying and classifying the snakes, lizards, salamanders, toads, frogs, and other specimens collected north of the Mexican boundary were an enormous undertaking that illustrated some important points. The project substantiated Baird's assessment of existing collections, catalogues, and monographs. In the one volume actually completed on North American reptiles, Baird and Girard identified and described almost three times as many species of North American snakes as had Holbrook.[16] But their *Catalogue of North American Reptiles: Serpents* (Volume 1) was more comprehensive because Smithsonian scientists had access to specimens unavailable to individual collectors like Holbrook.

4

Such lessons were not wasted on Baird. He had already recognized the important role that the government had played, and could continue to play, in the acquisition of scientific specimens. Soon after his marriage in 1846 to Mary Churchill, the daughter of Colonel Sylvester Churchill, he had his father-in-law supporting his passion for collecting by recruiting military personnel on his behalf, and before Baird was officially employed by the Smithsonian Institution in 1850, he obtained permission to "request of officers of the Army and Navy of the U. States and of other persons" that they collect natural history specimens for him in his future role as assistant secretary in charge of natural history.[17]

Authorization for Baird's plan to use military personnel in developing the Smithsonian natural history collections came from Joseph Henry, a renowned physicist and professor of natural philosophy at Princeton University who was appointed the first permanent secretary of the Smithsonian in 1846. Henry had well-defined priorities when it came to scientific matters. His biases in favor of research in the physical sciences and in favor of the publication of the results of original research were both known and accepted by the individuals who had supported his nomination for secretary.[18] The "intended object" of the Smithsonian was, in Henry's view, the development of collections that would permit original research while avoiding an unnecessary and expensive duplication of services provided by numerous other museums.[19]

Henry wanted any collections deposited at the Smithsonian to reflect the standards he had set for the Institution, to conform to scientific principles, and to have a bona fide and demonstrable scientific purpose. He deplored the notion of a chaotic collection of curiosities, and he ridiculed museums that consisted of "spectacular or bizarre objects with no scientific or educational value[, being] sideshows aimed at public gratification."[20] Convinced of Baird's commitment to original research, even if it was research in the natural sciences rather than the physical sciences, Henry put his new assistant in charge of securing research-oriented collections for the Smithsonian Institution.[21] Henry endorsed the distribution of a circular that Baird had written to solicit natural history specimens from individuals scattered throughout North America, and he approved Baird's plan to supply volunteer collectors with detailed instructions for fieldwork.[22]

Because improvements in the quality and quantity of collections could best be realized through the reform and regulation of previous collecting techniques and data gathering systems, Baird's instructions accompanied every important expedition dispatched by the U.S. government during the 1850s. Baird also outfitted the expeditions with collecting apparatus and materials, and he suggested names of qualified collectors to accompany the expeditions.[23] His ability to make collections through the American military superstructure meant that the Smithsonian natural history collections increased regularly and systematically. Because his instructions identified desiderata for zoological research, the chances of obtaining undesirable, exotic, or bizarre objects were reduced.

Until 1859 Baird's efforts at directing field collections focused on volunteers attached to government exploring expeditions; the majority of the specimens deposited at the Smithsonian Institution during the 1850s were collected by employees of the War Department, the Department of the Interior, the army, the navy, the Topographical Bureau, and various state surveys. Additions to the Smithsonian collections during the Civil War years came from another quarter, however. In 1858 Baird initiated an independent exploration program, and collections acquired between 1861 and 1866, under the auspices of the Smithsonian Explorations Program, provided specimens for research and display.[24] Baird first moved toward an independent Smithsonian program because antebellum explorations undertaken by the military concentrated on the midwestern and southern areas of the United States. Baird's natural history interests did not conform to the geographical limits of American military reconnaissance. He was also interested in the natural history of the far Northwest and of South America.

His field initiatives were well rewarded. The Smithsonian collections doubled despite the withdrawal of government support during the Civil War period. Antebellum accessions totaled 55,389, but Smithsonian collections exceeded 119,000 by 1866 as a result of Baird's program.[25] While the American government was preoccupied with wartime politics, military strategy, and reconstruction, specimens and data poured into the Smithsonian from Mexico, Guatemala, Ecuador, Costa Rica, Trinidad, Cuba, Jamaica, South America, and the Mackenzie River District of the Hudson's Bay Company's northern territories.[26]

Under Baird's supervision, Smithsonian-sponsored exploration quickly began to demonstrate its viability as a method of obtaining specimens. One of the most successful expeditions went to the Mackenzie River District. In April 1859, Robert Kennicott, a field naturalist from Illinois, left Chicago and made his way to Fort Simpson, the Hudson's Bay Company post at the fork of the Mackenzie and Liard rivers.[27] Kennicott was only 24 years old when he first went to arctic America, but his expedition initiated one of the most productive periods of natural history collecting in the territory known as Rupert's Land.[28] Moreover, one of the largest private collections the Smithsonian received during the 1860s was due to the efforts of the Hudson's Bay Company employees and northern native peoples recruited by Kennicott. During six collecting seasons, the Mackenzie River collectors submitted, on average, 1,700 specimens per year.[29] Zoological and anthropological specimens filling upwards of 20 cases and weighing approximately 1,000 pounds were sent out of the region every year from 1860 to 1866. The information that the collections provided on the animal populations and human inhabitants of the north was vastly superior to that of the peripatetic collections made during the previous 100 years.[30] The Mackenzie River collections not only verified earlier zoological lists and pre-ethnographic accounts on northern peoples but also added significantly to the empirical basis of the zoological and anthropological sciences in North America.

Kennicott was sent north because Baird was acutely aware that northern natural history collections were even less well developed than collections from temperate zones. In many cases, especially with regard to collections made by the Russians, Germans, and French in Russian America, descriptive accounts were all that attested to collections' having been made. The same was true for British collections. The Royal Society and the British Museum had received specimens from North America through the Hudson's Bay Company, as had the Natural History Society of Montreal and the University of Edinburgh, but only small numbers of specimens had been collected above the 60th parallel. Even fewer specimens still existed by the 1850s. Natural history specimens collected by Dr. John Rae while searching for the missing Franklin expedition between 1846 and 1849 had survived in the British Museum, but many specimens collected only 30 years earlier at York Factory by the first Franklin expedition had been lost or destroyed. So had many other specimens referred to in official Hudson's Bay Company documents and scientific works.[31] Overseas governor George Simpson, the Hudson's Bay Company's chief executive officer in North America, had established a private natural history museum at his home in Lachine, Quebec, but the extent to which he collected specimens before 1850 is uncertain.[32] Although references to northern specimens had been included in the scientific literature since the mid-eighteenth century, information on specifically North American specimens was as elusive as the collections themselves.

In addition, by 1850, new standards were being established for scientific research and publication. Never before had naturalists been so insistent that publications and research rest on hard data. The few available sources of information on northern plants and animals fell well short of standards that equated verification with scientific legitimacy. Most of the earlier natural history publications were based on data that were secondhand or that could not be verified through extant collections. Although such publications were cited regularly, they were never accepted uncritically; research undertaken by Baird and his associates was later praised because it demanded "exactitude in matters of fact, conciseness in deductive statement, and careful analysis of the subject in all its various bearings" and was "marked by a careful separation of the data from the conclusions derived from them, so that conclusions or arguments can be traced back to their sources and duly weighed."[33]

Baird and his contemporaries revered fieldwork. They acknowledged that zoological literature played an important role in scientific research, but they criticized the taxonomies constructed by the "closet naturalists," who based their work on secondhand or thirdhand bibliographic data irrespective of empirical data.[34] In Baird's opinion, species that had been described elsewhere but were not available for examination could not, in good conscience,

be included in catalogues or monographs associated with the Smithsonian Institution.

As Baird examined northern specimens deposited at the Smithsonian, the empirical lacunae became even more obvious. John Gould, a renowned British ornithologist, had sent from the British Museum approximately 150 avian specimens—a number of which were arctic specimens—but his collection was suggestive rather than representative or useful for zoological research.[35] The natural history specimens brought back by the Ringgold and Rodgers expedition in 1856 hinted at the potential of the north for collections and research, as did the specimens collected in northern Greenland by the Kane expedition of 1853 and the specimens collected between 1857 and 1859 along the southern border of present-day British Columbia by the North West Boundary Survey Commission. In total, the Smithsonian's northern collections represented little more than a foretaste of the riches of the peripheries of arctic America.[36]

Neither European nor American collections could support taxonomic or systematic studies of northern plants and animals, even though northern specimens had been collected sporadically for at least a century. Additional collections from northern North America were thus essential to further studies of speciation, zoological demographics, and systematics and to classificatory revisions proposed by North American taxonomists. But northern collections were important for another reason as well. Between 1850 and 1870, Smithsonian scientists substituted a cogent collecting program for the often erratic and unreliable system that had filled cabinets previously, and the Hudson's Bay Company traders and northern native collectors were part of that program. Guidelines were introduced in an attempt to ensure that all relevant specimens and data were collected, conserved, and recorded according to prescribed techniques. The scientific community was in the process of redefining data collection so that specimens and data fit its needs and criteria. The fieldworkers who were recruited on Kennicott's first northern expedition collected and processed their specimens in accordance with parameters being developed by a scientific community that was as concerned with rigor and replicability as it was with rarities.

The Mackenzie River collections were therefore important substantively, but they also demonstrated that Baird's rationalization of antebellum data-gathering systems could work. The Smithsonian's first foray into the north not only yielded enormous amounts of zoological and anthropological data—data that would form a significant component of the empirical basis of late nineteenth-century scientific research—but also tested the efficacy of controlled fieldwork and its applicability to modern science. Field studies were being defined, at least theoretically, by standards established by the scientific community responsible for processing the raw data, and the Mackenzie River collectors were important participants in the methodological reorientation from serendipitous to systematic data collection. In 1859 Baird was fortunate to find a group of men and women who were so responsive to the Smithsonian's specimen needs and so receptive to the overtures of his representative in the field, Robert Kennicott. In 1865, when Kennicott returned north to Russian America, Baird was not so lucky. Although Baird was able to introduce an element of control into field procedures, he could not control the conditions his workers found afield.

PART ONE

The Natural Sciences at the Smithsonian, 1850–1870

I

❦

A NORTH AMERICAN
ORIENTATION

The Smithsonian Institution was created in 1846 by an act of the
United States Congress, and almost from the beginning it functioned as a repository for scientific collections. According to Smithsonian scientists, they had the biggest and the best collection of
North American natural history specimens as early as 1855: "[O]n
the authority of Professor Baird, corroborated by the opinion of
others well qualified to judge, . . . no collection of animals in the
United States, nor, indeed, in the world, can even now pretend to
rival the richness of the museum of the Smithsonian Institution in
specimens which tend to illustrate the natural history of the continent of North America."[1]

The Smithsonian was admittedly at the forefront of the collecting mania that swept through the nineteenth-century scientific
community, but when Spencer Baird suggested that the Smithsonian "gather up such materials for investigation as have been
comparatively neglected by others,"[2] he was describing the first
stage of a comprehensive vision of the Institution's purpose:

> There certainly is no way in which the will of the founder of the
> Smithsonian Institution as to the increase of knowledge can be
> more effectively carried out than in taking charge of what no indi-

vidual or even ordinary society could grasp. I consider the day as not very distant when many of the most interesting questions in natural and physical sciences shall be solved by the agencies set in motion by the Institution. . . . I have long dreamed of some central association or influence which might call for such information, digest it, and then publish it in practical form to the world, and I see that my dream is not far from realization.[3]

Collections were undoubtedly important indexes of institutional repute, but in Baird's view they were never intended simply to satisfy acquisitive tendencies. They were also integral to basic research. Many North American plants and animals were still unknown to scientists; only the most preliminary steps in the identification, classification, and cataloguing of North American flora and fauna had been completed; and questions regarding geographical distribution, clinal variation, and the relationships among the plants, animals, climate, and topography of an ecosystem were in the formative stages. Data and specimens were essential for descriptive and enumerative studies, for comparative and analytical research, and for synthetic works.

One of the most productive and learned naturalists of his generation, Baird not only drew together the collections needed for scientific investigation but also was actively engaged in zoological research throughout the 37 years he was employed by the Smithsonian. When the ornithological collections at the Institution quadrupled between 1858 and 1864, he undertook work that led to the *Review of North American Birds* (1864–66) in order to provide identifications and technical descriptions for species not included in his *Catalogue of North American Birds* (1858) or its expanded reprints (1859, 1862).[4] Moreover, he quickly added analyses of geographical distribution and variation to his technical taxonomies. Two of Baird's most important works, *A History of North American Birds: Land Birds* (1874) and *The Water Birds of North America* (1884), contained information on life cycles and avian behavior, as well as detailed descriptions of identifying characteristics, range of distribution, and number of specimens examined. As a leading North American zoologist, Baird also wrote a series of articles during the 1860s on the geographical distribution, clinal variations, and migrations of North American birds.[5] In recognition of his many contributions to American science, Baird was made the first U.S. commissioner of fisheries in 1871 and the second secretary of the Smithsonian in 1878.

Although Baird's reputation as a scientist came to be identified with his ornithological work, the foundations of that reputation lay in some of his earliest projects. Even as a youth, Baird had collected and identified natural history specimens. He had published preliminary lists of birds (1843; 1845), trees and shrubs (1845), and amphibians (1849), as well as instructions for preparing natural history specimens (1846), prior to his Smithsonian appointment.[6] His reputation as a serious collector was one of the reasons Henry chose Baird as assistant secretary, and Baird's private cabinet, donated to the Smithsonian when he joined it in 1850, made up a large percentage of the Institution's early natural history collections.[7] But Baird was more than a collector. As assistant secretary in charge of the Natural History Department, he reported on collections made by the various boundary and transcontinental railroad surveys; he processed and analyzed the specimens and data deposited at the Smithsonian, personally identifying and cataloguing the mammalian and reptilian specimens; and he facilitated the publication of catalogues and reports on everything from beetles to fishes by loaning Smithsonian specimens to North American and European zoologists. He also collaborated with Charles Girard on an ophidian catalogue, and with ornithologists John Cassin and George N. Lawrence on a catalogue of North American birds.

Like most nineteenth-century naturalists, Baird was a taxonomist and a systematist. In many ways his first big assignment at the Smithsonian epitomized his career as a scientist.[8] Soon after his arrival, Baird assumed responsibility for the identification and classification of the herpetological specimens. His early work on reptiles reflected his strengths as a microtaxonomist. He focused on the delineation of species, genera, and families rather than debating ordinal classifications, and he added to or revised authoritative taxonomies only after exhaustive analyses:

[W]hen the great collection of snakes, containing several thousand specimens, was taken up for study, each specimen was individualized by attaching a number tag, which served as a key to its locality. They were all then thrown into one great pile, and by a process of comparison with absolute disregard for what had previously been written, assorted, first into families, then into genera, and then into species and varieties. After this had been done, descriptions and analytical keys were prepared and provisional names were given to each. Last of all, the books were consulted in order to determine which of them had already been described and provided with names.[9]

Serious researchers could test the empirical and textual basis of Baird and Girard's reptilian taxonomy. The accession numbers assigned to individual specimens were listed in the catalogue, and the specimens used in the identification of each species were retained in the Smithsonian collections.

Baird's work was not without opposition, however. A cordial and cooperative relationship with Louis Agassiz of Harvard University was adversely and irrevocably affected by Baird and Girard's *Catalogue of North American Reptiles* (1853). Agassiz questioned Baird's judgment as a taxonomist, disputing the validity of the morphological characters Baird had chosen to identify reptilian species. Agassiz also criticized the consistency and accuracy of Baird's nomenclature.[10]

Traditionally snakes had been grouped into poisonous and non-poisonous genera, but to classify North American snakes, Baird used morphological criteria such as the presence/absence and number of loreals, the roughness/smoothness and size of scales, and the mobility/immobility of teeth.[11] Agassiz took exception to Baird's willingness to ignore what he considered to be the natural divisions between venomous and nonvenomous snakes, and he especially objected to Baird's decision to place the poisonous coral snake (*Elaps fulvius*) in the Colubridae family.

Agassiz's criticisms of Baird's nomenclature were equally censorious. Accusations that Baird arbitrarily renamed species, misused the Greek alphabet, paired feminine nouns with masculine adjectives, and contravened the principle of priority indicated an aversion to the underlying premises of Baird's reptilian taxonomy no less than they questioned Baird's technical competency:

Have you noticed that your nomenclature makes it appear as if Europe and America had no two serpents allied even generically? Or is that a new theoretic view inferred by Girard from the *Astaci* which he believed to differ throughout generically and in structure from those of Europe? Shall next our Foxes in Europe and America be generically distinct? our Squirrels? our Rabbits & Hares? Such might be the inferences a geographer studying the geographical distribution of species in Europe and America would derive from your book compared with the works published in Europe. [12]

Philosophically, Agassiz could not condone the environmentalist viewpoint that prompted Baird to substitute specifically North American generic designations for Old World names. Agassiz contended that the existence of members of a genus in geographically disparate areas reflected separate but identical creations according to a divine plan. [13] He did not believe that environmental factors could modify the essential characteristics of organisms, and he could not understand why, for example, Baird would replace *Cenchris,* the Old World name for copperheads, with *Agkistrodon.*

Unintimidated, Baird responded to Agassiz's accusations. He justified his ophidian taxonomy on the basis that it represented a thorough examination and analysis of both the empirical evidence and the scientific literature. Baird was convinced of the validity of his judgments, stating emphatically, *"I do not believe that any genera of serpents are common to the two continents."* [14]

The dispute between Baird and Agassiz appeared superficial, but it reflected fundamental differences in their approaches to the natural sciences. Although Agassiz was famous for his lectures and essays on the relationships between God and the natural world, Baird's speculations were less lofty. Baird was less concerned with theoretical or philosophical issues than with practical results. His research, for the most part, focused on the taxonomic relationships among species, genera, and families, and so did his generalizations.

The rather cautious, often implicit, and empirically based hypotheses that characterized Baird's work on reptiles were equally typical of his mammalian and ornithological work. The practicalities of processing large numbers of specimens, as well as the strain placed upon existing classification systems by new information, again resulted in modified taxonomies. Baird was working with collections that exceeded most used previously in North America. Such an expanded data base allowed him not only to increase the number of snake species known to science but also to describe more than 200 new avian species and 70 new mammalian species. It also necessitated an extension and reorganization of the classificatory system used during the 1830s, 1840s, and even 1850s.[15] Baird sometimes multiplied and sometimes subdivided avian and mammalian genera to facilitate the identification of the many new specimens arriving at the Smithsonian.[16] He added, for example, 1 new genus and 7 new subgenera to existing mammalian classificatory schemes, and he added 19 genera and 2 subgenera to Audubon's avian classification.[17]

Baird's reorganizations were not always definitive, but they were a reflection of a conceptual change occurring among taxonomists. Modified taxonomies were constructed using modified methods of classification, and the upward, or compositional, method of classification—or a variation of it—was adopted by naturalists like Baird.[18] Although the downward, or divisional, method of classification provided a cogent and comprehensive means of hierarchically ordering the natural world, its reliance on single character differences made the realistic identification and classification of the numerous plant and animal species collected by nineteenth-century naturalists impossible. Distinctions among kingdoms, phyla, or classes were no longer an issue by 1850, whereas the identification and classification of individual species were of considerable importance. Baird tended to conceptualize classification as a logical progression downward from the general to the specific, but he did not adhere to the divisional, or dichotomous, method when he actually identified and grouped species into genera and families. Confronted with hundreds of specimens in his workroom, Baird based his identifications on as many morphological and anatomical criteria as possible, following for the most part the method of upward classification, which "starts at the bottom, sorts species into groups of similar ones, and combines these groups into a hierarchy of higher taxa."[19]

Another important component of Baird's taxonomic revisions was his reform and rationalization of scientific nomenclature. The pitfalls of taxonomic synonymy had been recognized as early as the

1820s when Charles L. Bonaparte's attempts at avian identification and classification were confounded by the existence of several scientific names,[20] but Baird was one of the first naturalists to review exhaustively a wide range of zoological literature before naming specimens. Adopting Bonaparte's methodology, he assumed the tedious task of ferreting out often obscure references for the many different names given North American taxa, determining the priority among them, and assigning one scientific name. In his 1859 *Catalogue of North American Birds,* for example, Baird adopted the name *Zonotrichia albicollis* for the white-throated sparrow. That scientific name had been given to the bird by Bonaparte in 1850 and was later adopted by the American Ornithologists' Union.[21] Baird chose *Zonotrichia albicollis* over *Passer pennsylvanicus* (Brisson, 1760), *Fringilla albicollis* (Gmelin, 1788; Wilson, 1811), *Fringilla pennsylvanica* (Latham, 1790; Audubon, 1831), *Fringilla (Zonotrichia) pennsylvanica* (Swainson, 1831), and *Zonotrichia pennsylvanica* (Bonaparte, 1838) because, according to the principle of priority, neither ordinal designations (Passeres) nor family names (Fringillidae) may be used to name an individual species.[22] The species name (*albicollis*) first given the white-throated sparrow by Gmelin, and later paired with *Zonotrichia* by Bonaparte, was retained because it had chronological priority over any other designation.

Baird unswervingly adhered to Bonaparte's dictum because, until the mid-nineteenth century, species often had several scientific names. The Linnaean system failed to regulate the derivation and application of scientific names; thus the Latinized binomes given plants and animals were almost as idiosyncratic and colloquial as their common counterparts.[23] Baird replaced erroneous, idiosyncratic, or arbitrary designations with names that adhered strictly to the principle of priority, and his notes distinguished between vernacular and scientific terminology. Baird retained geographical, morphological, and even honorific designations, but he agreed with other reformers that names derived from mythology, history, or the Bible were inappropriate.[24]

More specifically, Baird's later ornithological catalogues and monographs were also representative of changes associated with the development of an international system of nomenclature. In

1889 the First International Congress of Zoology called for an international system of zoological nomenclature based on the trinomial system that had been advocated by members of the Bairdian school of ornithology, especially Elliott Coues and Robert Ridgway, and had been adopted by the American Ornithologists' Union (AOU) in 1885. An international code of zoological nomenclature was not actually realized until 1961, but the code that was finally accepted incorporated the trinomen formally adopted by the AOU to indicate species variation or subspecies.[25] In conformity with the AOU system, subspecies were designated by a trinomen, species were designated by a binomen, and all the higher categories— genus, family, order, and class—were given uninomial designations.

Before 1885, American ornithologists, especially members of the Bairdian school, used a modified binomial system to indicate species variation.[26] Adopting the system introduced by Coues in *Key to North American Birds* (1872), Baird, for example, named a regionally distinct variety of the screech owl *Scops asio* var. *kennicottii* [*Otus asio kennicottii*] in his *History of North American Birds* (1874). Other regionally distinct species were also named in conformity with Coues's system, and individuals accorded species status in Baird's earlier catalogues were reduced to subspecies or varieties after 1872. In the early 1880s Robert Ridgway, one of the collaborators on the *History of North American Birds,* converted the modified binomial system used in the *History* into a truly trinomial system by omitting the qualifier "var."[27]

Trinomialism had some obvious advantages, but the scientific community was less than unanimous in its acceptance of the AOU system of nomenclature. Although trinomials replaced the cumbersome practice of denoting subspecies with a third Latin name prefaced by the term "variety," many taxonomists nevertheless disputed the validity and usefulness of the American system. Some scientists accepted trinomialism but disputed the AOU criteria for determining subspecies status; others rejected the underlying premises of the system. Thus, several systems of nomenclature appeared in the second half of the nineteenth century. National codes were advanced by the Société Zoologique de France (1881) and the Deutsche Zoologische Gesellschaft (1894), and the Dall

Code of the American Association for the Advancement of Science predated the AOU Code by eight years. British zoologists remained staunch supporters of the binomial system, resisting changes to the rules worked out by Hugh Strickland and adopted by the British Association for the Advancement of Science in 1842.[28]

The AOU system rested on positive correlations among geography, morphology, and species variation. Evidence for those correlations was supplied by naturalists such as Baird who increasingly applied their talents to studies of species variation and the phenomena of cline. Like other naturalists, Baird subscribed to a typological species definition based on morphological and anatomical criteria, but the Smithsonian collections allowed him to examine several specimens of a single species. Not only did he recognize that individual differences existed within a species taxon, but he also attempted to describe, quantify, and explain those differences in terms of adaptation. Access to zoological specimens from almost every region of North America, as well as to climatological data from the Smithsonian Meteorological Program and geographical data from the various government surveys, enabled Baird to analyze the relationship between morphology and geography with a great deal of confidence and to substantiate theories proposed by European ornithologists Carl Bergmann and Constantin Lambert Gloger.[29] The differences Baird observed in body size between specimens from the far north and those collected south of the international boundary, as well as differences found in the size of individuals living in mountainous regions and members of the same species living at lower altitudes, confirmed Bergmann's hypothesis that body size increases with decreasing temperatures. Similarly, access to Pacific Coast and inland specimens of the same species convinced Baird that plumage tends to darken with increased humidity (Gloger's Rule).

New data also allowed Baird to anticipate the work of future North American systematists, especially his student J. A. Allen.[30] Although the Bairdian school of ornithology leaned toward the theory of acquired characteristics rather than natural selection as the most probable explanation of how speciation occurred in the geographically disparate regions of North America, Baird was less certain than Allen about the relationship between geography and the size of avian extremities.[31] Some of Baird's findings supported Allen's assertions that bills, tails, and other body extensions would be longer in warm climates than in cooler climates, but Baird also had contradictory evidence. Baird, like Allen, found some southern birds to have larger bills than their northern counterparts, but he found an east-west rather than a north-south variation in tail length.

Baird's studies of morphology and anatomy were unrelated to Allen's work, however, and played a coincidental, though important, role in the eventual refutation of Allen's theory.[32] Always the practical naturalist, Baird looked for the taxonomic significance of correlations among geography, morphology, and speciation rather than emphasizing their purely predictive value. He used the information provided by systematics for the identification of species, not for classificatory or ontological purposes: "Both these generalizations in regard to varieties of size and proportion have been used with advantage in testing the claim of supposed species to this rank, and have aided in materially diminishing the accepted number of species of both mammals and birds."[33]

Baird's belief that research into zoological systematics would reduce the propensity of naturalists to "discover" new species was overconfident, though. American scientists were as likely to multiply species taxa as they were to reduce the number of species already identified. Baird, Brewer, and Ridgway, for example, erroneously classified the common gyrfalcon (*Falco rusticolus*) into three subspecies based on seasonal variation rather than on geographically distinct coloration: *Falco gyrfalco* var. *canadicans* (white phase), var. *labradora* (black phase), and var. *sacer* (brown phase).[34] By subdividing *Falco rusticolus,* they increased the number of species taxa, but technically they were not species splitters, because they had refrained from assigning species status to each phase. Rather than being lumpers, though, they were simply incorrect. Such errors unfortunately exacerbated and formalized an ongoing dispute between splitters and "lumpers" that no amount of systematic research seemed able to resolve.[35]

Analyses of geographical distribution and variation took scientists in other directions as well. Systematists were inevitably led to zoogeography, and both Baird and J. A. Allen were noted zoogeographers. In 1865, just six years before Allen drafted a zoological map rejecting the one proposed by the famous European ornithologist Philip Sclater, Baird critiqued Sclater's work.[36] Unlike Allen, Baird agreed with Sclater's general conclusions, disputing certain features of Sclater's map but not his fundamental propositions. Whereas Allen substituted latitudinally based zoological regions for Sclater's Old World and New World divisions, Baird agreed with Sclater that the fauna of the Old World differed fundamentally from that of the New World. Baird also concurred with Sclater's subdivision of the Old World into three zoological regions, but he disputed Sclater's delineation of the New World into two zoological regions. Instead, Baird divided the New World into three regions—North America, South America, and the West Indies. He then divided the North American, or Nearctic, region into eastern and western provinces and subdivided the western province to create a middle province. Both Baird and Sclater based their zoogeographical conclusions on avian data, but although Baird's division of North America into three zoological provinces was generally accepted, his tripartite division of the New World proved less enduring than Sclater's earlier schema. Baird's efforts were nevertheless typical of a generation of taxonomists and systematists who were trying to make sense out of the vast amount of empirical data at their disposal.

The Smithsonian collections making up Baird's expanded data base facilitated basic research in herpetology, mammalogy, ichthyology, conchology, entomology, mineralogy, paleontology, archaeology, ethnology, osteology, and embryology, as well as in ornithology and oology,[37] but merely having such collections meant that considerable time had already been invested. Although collecting specimens could be interesting, it was also exacting, time-consuming, and even tedious. Fieldworkers were therefore often reminded of the crucially important role that they played in the extension of the zoological sciences, and none more so than the collectors residing in the far northern outposts of the Mackenzie River District.

Large collections were appreciated for their distributive and augmentative functions, but northern collections were also important because they verified the data contained in contemporary treatises on northern natural history and because research on the distribution, migration, and breeding habits of North American animals would be incomplete and inconclusive without specimens from the most remote, as well as the most accessible, parts of the continent. Robert Kennicott assured northern collectors of the importance of their specimens to the advancement of science: "You must observe that in most cases it is not the intrinsic value of the specimens themselves (for I will own that most of the specimens are *necessarily* in a d——nable condition from being carried where you had no conveniences—) that renders them so important but their ability to tell us the story of Arctic zoology is what renders your collection so valuable to science."[38] The Mackenzie River collectors responded enthusiastically to such earnest assessments of their contributions.

By 1860 Baird had moved the avian sciences to the forefront of the research and collections programs in the Natural History Department, and northern specimens and data were essential to studies of the relationship between climate and morphology, to taxonomic identifications, and to studies of the geographical distribution and migration of North American species. To facilitate and organize his work in systematics and taxonomy, Baird divided the continent into seven regions based on avian breeding grounds: (1) North America as a whole, (2) British North America east of the Rocky Mountains, (3) the northern and northeastern seaboard, (4) the middle region of eastern North America, (5) the southern region of eastern North America, (6) the Rocky Mountains and adjacent plains, and (7) the Pacific Coast. But as Baird pointed out, few locations could surpass the north for data on North American oology: "It is in this region, especially among the water birds breeding in the more northern portion towards Russian America and Behring's Straits, that the greatest number of deficiencies in the Smithsonian oological collection is to be found. From the mouth of the Columbia northward, every kind of egg, whether of land or water bird, will be an acceptable addition to the series."[39] All specimens were acceptable acquisitions, but the many birds and eggs sent south by northerners were particularly important to avian systematics and taxonomy. Kennicott was sent north to bring back specimens from those rich breeding grounds.

Northern birds eggs were also of special interest to Thomas Mayo Brewer, a noted oologist who was working through the Smithsonian natural history and publications programs on a multi-volume study entitled *North American Oology*. Like the other members of the Bairdian school, Brewer disdained the work of those individuals who were referred to as closet naturalists, and he refused to include drawings of eggs that were based on other people's illustrations or to reproduce drawings of eggs that were unavailable for physical inspection. Moreover, Brewer was not content to illustrate eggs after examining just one specimen. He suggested that upwards of 50 specimens of a single species be collected and that those specimens depict the various stages of embryonic development. He was convinced that both external morphology and embryological development provided useful classificatory criteria, and he wanted to obtain multiple specimens in order to test oological data as a means of identifying avian species.[40]

Brewer's belief that taxonomists and systematists required large numbers of eggs for their research could certainly be tested after 1860. Northern collections were especially rich in oological specimens. But northerners also sent birds, fishes, reptiles, amphibians, insects, and shells.[41] Many mammals, particularly the fur-bearing animals traded at Hudson's Bay Company posts, were sent to the Smithsonian. The skins and skeletons of marten, mink, beaver, foxes, and wolves were accompanied by specimens of mice, shrews, moose, caribou, buffalo, mountain goats, and Indian dogs. Collections of mammal skulls were often sent independently, and the embryos of mammals, birds, and other animals were sent when available. Geological specimens, including minerals, rocks, and fossils, made up a small percentage of the packets sent south, as did botanical specimens. Examples of native clothing and artwork, as well as the tool kits of a number of native cultural groups, also arrived at the Smithsonian.

The collections from the north reflected the diversity of the interests that Baird pursued, and they proved that his vision of the Smithsonian was feasible. But his ability to secure specimens from such a remote region of North America also demonstrated his administrative talents and his ingenuity and expertise as a data collector. By 1860 the Smithsonian's field of operations had expanded from the eastern seaboard to the western coast, and from Mexico and the West Indies to the far northern fringes of the continent. The natural history collections contained upwards of 250,000 individual specimens,[42] and Baird concentrated his energies on managing the Natural History Department and the tasks associated with acquiring and processing data and specimens.[43]

BAIRD'S ADVANCES IN FIELDWORK

Baird's assessment of the empirical deficiencies of the natural sciences in North America was combined with a critical examination of field methods. Obtaining the number of specimens required for the Smithsonian natural history museum and for basic research would have been impossible without improved data gathering techniques.

When Baird joined the Institution, field methods were rudimentary. Specimens were collected irregularly, and the procedures followed by field collectors were at times counterproductive. For example, many collectors still identified new specimens through comparison with previously processed specimens. That practice, as Baird observed, had unfortunate ramifications for both curators and researchers: "Hitherto, officers of the army returning to Washington have generally been obliged to send or carry these objects out of the city, for the purpose of identification or verification, thus involving a considerable loss of time and credit. These specimens becoming widely scattered, rarely return hither, and when another occasion arises, the whole labor has to be repeated."[1] Increased accessions were impossible so long as fieldworkers used preserved and labeled specimens instead of catalogues or checklists as identification aids. In addition, it became increasingly impractical to send type specimens to identify specimens collected in the remote regions of North America that were visited by government and Smithsonian-sponsored expeditions. Baird therefore used his position as assistant secretary of the Smithsonian to reform and regulate fieldwork.

The exigencies of collecting specimens far from the scrutiny of experts, as well as the deleterious effects of distributing previously processed specimens, convinced Baird of the necessity and the practicality of a series of zoological catalogues and checklists. Catalogues could be taken afield for identifying specimens, and collectors were instructed to record their observations according to the format found in Baird's catalogues.[2] Although catalogues and checklists allowed field collectors to tentatively identify their specimens with an unprecedented degree of confidence and without jeopardizing existing collections, well-preserved and properly processed specimens were required so that catalogues and checklists could be compiled. Baird therefore juggled the preparation of catalogues with a comprehensive collecting program. Zoological taxonomies were revised and expanded as new data became available, and instructional pamphlets were refined and reissued regularly. By 1860 Baird had supervised the preparation of several specialized pamphlets on the collection and preservation of natural history specimens, in addition to preparing a pamphlet of general instructions entitled "Directions for Collecting, Preserving, and Transporting Specimens of Natural History" (1851).[3] His success at replacing existing field practices by a reformed and rationalized data gathering system was recognized formally when the Smithsonian Miscellaneous Collections series was begun in the 1860s "to facilitate the various branches of natural history, to give instruction as to the method of observing phenomena, and to furnish a variety of other matter connected with the progress of science."[4]

Neither institutional pride nor scientific research could condone second-rate collections. In Baird's opinion, collecting and processing specimens were serious undertakings. His instructions were therefore prefaced by a statement of the principles, policies, and procedures acceptable for the research and display programs of the Natural History Department:

The general principle to be observed in making collections of Natural History, especially in a country but little explored, is to gather all the species which may present themselves, subject to the convenience or practicability of transportation. The number of specimens to be secured will, of course, depend upon their size, and the variety of form or condition caused by the different features of age, sex, or season.

As the object of the Institution in making its collections is not merely to possess the different species, but also to determine their geographical distribution, it becomes important to have as full series as practicable from each locality. And in commencing such collections, the commonest species should be secured first, as being most characteristic, and least likely to be found elsewhere. It is a fact well known in the history of museums, that the species which from their abundance would be the first expected, are the last to be received.

In every little known region the species which are the commonest, are rarest elsewhere, and many an unscientific collector in Texas, Mexico, the Rocky Mts., and elsewhere, has been surprised to find what he considered the least valuable species in his collection (owing to the ease with which they had been obtained in numbers), more prized by the naturalist than the rarities, which were in fact only well known stragglers from more accessible localities.

The first specimen procured of any animal, however imperfect, should be preserved, at least until a better can be obtained.

Where a small proportion only of the specimens collected can be transported, such species should be selected as are least likely to be procured in other localities or on other occasions. Among these may be mentioned reptiles, fishes, soft insects, &c.; in short, all such as require alcohol for their preservation. Dried objects, as skins, can be procured with less difficulty, and are frequently collected by persons not specially interested in scientific pursuits.

In gathering specimens of any kind, it is important to fix with the utmost precision the localities where found. This is especially desirable in reference to fishes and other aquatic animals, as they occupy a very intimate relation to the waters in which they live.[5]

Although Baird's pamphlets were composed so as "to enable any one, with but little practice, to produce specimens sufficiently

well for the ordinary purposes of science," Baird avoided conde-
scension and provided straightforward instructions that left nothing to chance.[6] Lists of apparatus and preservatives were
accompanied by blank forms to accommodate the data that were
to describe preserved specimens. The pamphlets itemized the
kinds of specimens wanted by the Smithsonian: zoological specimens, including embryonic and osteological specimens; botanical
and geological specimens, including paleontological specimens;
and soils and sediments containing microscopic plants and animals. Baird described proper recording procedures and the recognized, as well as the practicable, preservation techniques for each
type of specimen in turn. Because specimens were often delicate
and had to travel many miles before arriving at the Smithsonian,
he also gave detailed instructions for their packing and shipping.

Baird provided graphic descriptions of preservation techniques,
particularly skinning and stuffing, along with straightforward and
practical instructions on the handling of zoological specimens, but
only cursory discussions of how to procure specimens were
included. Although Baird valued common sense, addressing even
the most mundane aspects of specimen preparation, he evidently
believed that intuition and ingenuity were the only assets required
for individuals engaged in hunting, trapping, and netting zoological specimens. Nothing was apparently more instructive to the
novice than experience in the field. Even the most preliminary
steps associated with natural history collecting were absent from
Baird's pamphlets. Once obtained, however, specimens had to be
processed according to recognized scientific standards.[7]

The routine preservation of ornithological and mammalian
specimens was similar enough to render repetition unnecessary in
Baird's "Directions." Virtually identical skinning techniques and
preservation procedures were, with two exceptions, followed for
both birds and mammals. Small specimens of either class were
treated with arsenic compounds, although a concoction of alum
and saltpeter was substituted for arsenic when treating the much
larger surface areas of most mammal skins. Both mammal and bird
specimens were susceptible to larval damage, but the larger skins
required more radical treatment not only because of their size but
also because the hair, wool, and fur covering them was highly

susceptible to gnats. Larval damage rendered specimens useless as research and display skins, wasting the many hours invested in collection, preservation, and packing. Once specimens had been infiltrated by larvae, eradication of the pests was impossible. Organic materials such as wool, hair, and feathers were therefore never to be used as stuffing or packing materials, because they were often contaminated with insect eggs. Irreparable damage could be averted only if insects were kept away from the stuffed specimens, and healthy doses of creosote, ether, chloroform, turpentine, and tobacco leaves were also applied to mammal skins as a precaution.

The necessity for wet preservation made fishes and other marine specimens the most difficult specimens to process and ship out of the north. Plants, minerals, and fossils were, on the other hand, the easiest specimens to collect and process, though not always the easiest to transport. Satisfactory botanical collections could be made simply by pressing specimens between folios and ensuring that each was accompanied by adequate notation. Similarly, minerals and fossils required little exertion or expertise, beyond that associated with labeling and packing. Crumbling fossils required some attention, but few collectors would resort to the efforts required to mend a fossil by soaking it in glue or melted wax when fossils were easily obtained.

An interest in geographical distribution, combined with an awareness of the propensity of collectors to favor unusual or rare varieties over the common species, made Baird sensitive to the necessity of representative sampling and led him toward an elementary form of biometrics.[8] Because his identifications and classifications were made by examining as many specimens as possible and by examining several morphological characteristics, he suggested that collectors capture numerous specimens in each taxon of both common and rare species. The advantages of large collections were made clear when Baird and Girard worked on the ophidian catalogue, identifying 130 North American species after examining several thousand snakes, and Baird anticipated the utility of large collections for other zoological research.

Baird also saw the potential for finding data in unusual places. He stipulated that collectors include all of their observations, no matter how trivial, and that no source of specimens be overlooked.

For example, the contents of the gastrointestinal tracts of dead animals and the parasites found on host carcasses were as useful to science as was the primary specimen. Baird pointed out, however, that the value of such specimens, like all others, decreased if they were submitted without data on their locality, date of capture, habits and peculiarities, sex, and body measurements. He continually emphasized the importance of accurate labeling throughout the collecting process. Knowing that notes were useful on their own account, Baird pleaded with collectors to record their observations in the field diligently and to compile lists of species sighted but not collected. Baird also stressed that record keeping, as well as collecting, could be facilitated through consultation with indigenous inhabitants, who often had an extensive knowledge of local resources. Their comments were always to be included in field notes.

Baird's first set of instructions provided elementary directions for the collection and preservation of all natural history specimens, but the increasing tendency toward specialization in the sciences, the uneven development of zoological data bases, and the interests of the zoologists and naturalists themselves prompted the publication of specialized instructions. For example, entomology, like so many areas within the zoological sciences in North America, lagged behind European studies. The Smithsonian therefore attempted to promote North American entomological research by printing directions explaining where the different types of insects could be found, how to capture them, and how to preserve and transport them. Nationally and internationally recognized experts provided instructions in 1858. Directions for the collection and preservation of Hymenoptera (ants, bees, wasps, and sawflies), Orthoptera (earwigs, cockroaches, locusts, crickets, and grasshoppers), Hemiptera (bugs), Neuroptera (lacewings, ant lions, alderflies, and scorpionflies), Coleoptera (beetles), Diptera (flies, gnats, and midges), and Lepidoptera (butterflies and moths) were prepared by John LeConte, a trained physician from Philadelphia who became an expert on Coleoptera; Baron Carl Osten Sacken, a member of the Russian diplomatic service in North America and an expert on Diptera; Brackinridge Clemens, an expert on Lepidoptera from Easton, Pennsylvania; Hermann Loew, an entomologist from Vienna; and Philip Uhler, an entomologist from Baltimore.[9] Their directions were printed in the Smithsonian *Annual Report.*

By the late 1850s Baird had developed a special interest in ornithology, and Thomas Mayo Brewer, who was already a noted oologist, prominent Bostonian businessman, and publisher, wrote "Instructions in Reference to Collecting Nests and Eggs of North American Birds" (1858) for the Smithsonian.[10] Brewer's pamphlet was reissued several times, appearing in advance of the 1861 collecting season with two attachments: a circular from Baird indicating the species needed to complete Brewer's oological work, and an article by an English oologist, Alfred Newton, on the preparation of eggs. The species needed for the forthcoming *History of North American Birds* were listed; vultures, hawks, owls, woodpeckers, warblers, jays, ducks, geese, sandpipers, and auks were particularly desired, although Baird noted that the Smithsonian had many other deficiencies in its oological collections.

Brewer requested that collectors obtain as many nests and eggs as possible during May and June, the best months for oological collecting. Nests required little preservation beyond being carefully packed for transport, but the shells of the more delicate eggs had to be emptied, cleaned, and labeled. Baird and Brewer, as well as Newton, emphasized the importance of adhering strictly to accepted procedure in the emptying and preparation of eggs, but Newton went beyond general admonishments, providing readers with his philosophy on the "principal object[s]," or duties, of the egg collector to science.

Newton pointed out that oological specimens were virtually useless without reference to at least one parent for identification or, in the absence of an adult specimen, copious notes. Descriptions of habitat, locale, and nest structure, and estimates of the general bird population, had to be recorded to enable even tentative identifications. Observational evidence could, if necessary, substantiate oological identifications in the absence of ornithological corroboration. The validity of any such identifications depended, however, on the ability of scientists such as Newton and Baird to assess the reliability and competence of the field collectors, and such assessments depended on a reference point: self-identification. Oological collectors, regardless of their educational background, expertise, or experience, were to identify themselves clearly, thus fulfilling the requirements of a process Newton called authentication.

Baird and his collaborators—Brewer, Osten Sacken, LeConte, Loew, Clemens, and Newton—sought to introduce an element of design into fieldwork, improving upon the sporadic, primitive attempts at systematization found in the natural history handbooks and pamphlets of the previous two centuries. Instructions written by Pierre Belon (ca. 1517–1564) in 1555 for the preservation of bird skins, and suggestions given by John Woodward (1665–1728) in 1696 for "making observations in all parts of the world" were two of the earliest attempts to focus the activities of specimen collectors, but similar attempts were made throughout the eighteenth and nineteenth centuries.[11] James Petiver (1663–1718), a London apothecary, supplied explorers with preservatives and outlined the steps associated with stuffing birds for display. A French naturalist, René-Antoine Ferchault de Réaumur (1683–1757), similarly sent instructions with French travelers in order to add exotic specimens to his museum.[12] In *A Catalogue of the Animals of North America* (1771), John Reinhold Forster described the types of information relevant to identify captured species. *Traité 1674 élémentaire et complet d'ornithologie, ou histoire naturelle des oiseaux* (1800), by F. M. Daudin (1774–1804), suggested topics accessible through field observation; *Anatomie und Naturgeschichte der Vogel* (1810–14), by Friedrich Tiedemann (1781–1861), was Daudin's German equivalent. Standards for British field ornithology were established by George Montague's *Ornithological Dictionary* (two volumes, 1802 and 1813), and William Swainson wrote *Instructions for Collecting and Preserving Subjects of Natural History and Botany* (1808).

Baird was admittedly not the first person to prepare instructions for collecting and preserving natural history specimens, but his field instructions were more comprehensive than previous ones. He was more definitive when identifying the types of collections that he wanted and in giving instructions for the preparation of specimens. Because his manuals were used specifically to realize a comprehensive and long-term collections program, Baird aspired to and achieved an unprecedented degree of standardization and efficiency in data collection. Additionally, the Smithsonian Institution had the organizational structure, finances, and cohesiveness necessary to process the large numbers of specimens entrusted to it.[13] Baird's instructions were also distinguished from earlier ones by being widely and regularly distributed, accompanying as many as 65 exploratory and surveying expeditions dispatched by the U.S. government and as many as 110 Smithsonian-sponsored collecting expeditions between 1851 and 1870.[14]

Baird introduced changes into zoological fieldwork unparalleled since the late eighteenth century, when arsenical soap was invented. Arsenical soap was important to zoology because it was the first really effective preservative, allowing large-scale and longer-lasting collections.[15] But the collecting program that Baird supervised out of the Smithsonian dramatically increased the potential for making acquisitions based on late eighteenth-century technological advances. The Smithsonian collections grew quickly because Baird's collecting network was vast, and they were useful for research because Baird introduced a level of control into field projects that was previously impossible except when knowledgeable individuals did their own collecting.

Baird, like European scientists such as John Gray at the British Museum, acquired some natural history specimens through exchanges with other scientific institutions, but that source of specimens was limited by the size of the collections available for exchange and by the quality of the specimens being traded. Baird's ability to develop collections was limited in another way that most European repositories were not. Smithsonian funds and official policies prevented the purchase of specimens, whereas the British Museum, for example, which had the largest zoological collection in Europe in 1854, had obtained many specimens through purchase since 1840.[16] Because purchasing specimens was not possible at the Smithsonian, Baird had to devise ways of securing specimens as gifts from colleagues and other interested individuals. Such gifts could be a burden rather than a blessing, though. The idiosyncracies of collectors were more likely to be represented in collections dependent on gifts than were the needs of science. Unless scientists made their own collections, they could never guarantee that they would have the specimens they needed;

but without assistance, one person could not collect a comprehensive series of even one class of animals. Baird's great feat was that he substituted a cogent and sustained collecting program for the informal and ad hoc approach that had previously supplied scientists with specimens and data.

Within a decade, Baird's new approach to zoological data collection was extended into the rapidly expanding fields of ethnology and archaeology. Anthropology as a scientific discipline was just beginning to assume its modern form during the 1860s, and two of the most significant manifestations of that transformation were introduced by the systematization of fieldwork that developed under Baird's administration.[17] "Instructions for Archaeological Investigations in the U. States" and "Instructions Relative to the Ethnology and Philology of America," published by the Smithsonian Institution during the 1860s, anticipated the reorientation of a discipline, which, once established, rendered ad hoc donations obsolete.[18]

Descriptive accounts of non-European peoples living in remote or exotic locations had long been committed to paper out of curiosity, a fascination with the bizarre or unfamiliar, the desire to titillate and amuse the readers of travelogues, or the immeasurably practical and immediate purposes typical of accounts compiled by early fur traders, colonial administrators, and missionaries. But a new breed of scientist was emerging—the social scientist. During the first half of the nineteenth century, incipient social scientists recognized the limitations of ethnographic materials that had been collected for purposes either incompatible with or entirely unrelated to their interests. Their requirements for additional and more "objective" information led to the development of new collection techniques. Almost 14 years before the British Association for the Advancement of Science and the Anthropological Institute published *Notes and Queries* as a means of rationalizing data collection, the Smithsonian's anthropological instructions introduced direction and control into field procedures, ushering in an era in which the armchair anthropologist's reliance on incidental observation of indigenous cultures was replaced by systematic data collection.[19]

The new instructions, like those written by natural scientists during the previous decade, were predicated on an assumption that significant numbers of collectors would be at the disposal of professional scientists. A request for assistance from nonscientists thus prefaced the directions on anthropological fieldwork:

> The Smithsonian Institution is desirous of extending and completing its collections of facts and materials relative to the Ethnology, Archaeology, and Philology of the races of mankind inhabiting, either now or at any previous period, the continent of America, and earnestly solicits the cooperation in this object of all officers of the United States government, and travellers, or residents who may have it in their power to render any assistance.[20]

In the winter of 1865–66, when Robert Kennicott made his unsuccessful trip to Russian America on behalf of the Smithsonian, it became obvious that any attempt to reform or rationalize field methods in either the natural or the social sciences would be deferred, if not futile, in the absence of willing participants. Kennicott had been sent north to "work up" the natural history of Russian America, but few individuals were interested in his projects, and he received little institutional support; consequently, little was accomplished during his brief sojourn in Russian America. William Dall, Kennicott's assistant during 1865 and 1866, went on to become the "Dean of Alaskan Experts," but only after government interests in Alaska provided a framework and an incentive for natural history explorations. In 1859, however, the indigenous collectors that Kennicott recruited from within the Hudson's Bay Company and native communities in the far north played a decisive role in the methodological transformation associated with the Bairdian period of North American science. They had personal reasons for supporting Smithsonian science, and it was Baird's good fortune that Kennicott found such a highly motivated group of collectors in the Mackenzie River District. There were but few career scientists at midcentury; the institutionalization of science was just beginning. The northern collectors were crucial to Baird's collecting program, for it would be some time before scientific organizations employed significant numbers of individuals as field and laboratory assistants.

PART TWO

The Natural Sciences in Rupert's Land, 1859–1867

3

❧

KENNICOTT IN ARCTIC AMERICA

When Robert Kennicott headed north in 1859, he was determined to get to Russian America. He planned to collect extensively as he passed from post to post in the Hudson's Bay Company territories, but his ultimate destination was the northwesternmost portion of North America. By December 1860, however, Kennicott had abandoned his plan of going on to the Russian posts. He believed that he could make better collections at less expense while at Hudson's Bay Company posts, and he discovered that it was unfeasible to travel by land to the Russian coast: "I've given up all idea of trying the Russian posts, as the prospects are better elsewhere and I'm quite in the dark as to means of carrying on operations there—maybe within the next ten years we'll find ways & means to send me or some one else around by water!"[1]

The Mackenzie River District was ostensibly located within reach of three of the seven zoogeographical regions listed in Baird's circular on collecting nests and eggs—namely, the Rocky Mountains, the eastern foothills and plains, and the Pacific Coast—but overland access to those breeding grounds was much more limited than either Baird or Kennicott understood. Travel between the district and Russian America was not only impractical but also virtually impossible. Although the Hudson's Bay Company (HBC) had negotiated a free trade zone with the Russian American Company in 1839, HBC officials could not guarantee passage into Russian America, nor would they necessarily encourage communications with Russian traders. Kennicott quickly decided to focus on the Mackenzie River District. Because the natural history of the HBC's northern territories had received little serious study and because his plans to collect specimens in Rupert's Land were fully supported by the company, his decision was easily made.

When Joseph Henry originally requested permission to send Kennicott into the HBC's northern territories, his petition to the company was endorsed by Lord William Napier, the British ambassador to the United States.[2] Napier's support undoubtedly impressed HBC governor George Simpson, but the governor's endorsement also reflected past practice. The company had a long history of supporting scientific activities. Five of its 18 founding members, as well as Prince Rupert (the first governor) and several shareholders, were fellows of the Royal Society, and their scientific interests meant that HBC data on North American geography, meteorology, and terrestrial magnetism were made available to the society during the seventeenth and eighteenth centuries.[3] In the eighteenth century, the Hudson's Bay Company sanctioned and indeed encouraged its employees to collect natural history specimens in Rupert's Land:

> Wee must repeat our former Order that You at a Proper season plant in boxes some Roots of the several sorts of Herbs, Plants, Grass & shrubs that are in your parts and save at a proper season some of the seeds, Berries, Cones or Kernels of all growing in Your Country and send them to Us[.] [A]lso lett yr Surgeon give Us a particular Description thereof and their names and Qualities and what use the Natives put them to and send us an acctt in writing of the particulars of what You put on board of that kind[.] This Order wee require may not be neglected for the future.[4]

By 1772, sufficient numbers of specimens had been collected to warrant the creation of a committee to deal specifically with specimens received by the Royal Society from HBC employees in North America, and specimens collected in Rupert's Land were used by some of the most prominent eighteenth-century zoologists.[5]

Even though the company did all in its power to restrict access to Rupert's Land, it welcomed scientific visitors. In 1768, for example, an astronomer and mathematician named William Wales was permitted to stay at Fort Prince of Wales (Churchill) to document the parallax of the transit of Venus (3 June 1769) for the Royal Society. In the early nineteenth century, scientists and collectors were frequently allowed to explore the HBC's North American territories. David Douglas, a Scottish botanist who visited the northwestern United States in 1823 and again in 1830–33, traveled to the Fort Vancouver District in 1824–27 and to Red River in 1827.[6] Karl Andreas Geyer, the editor of the *London Journal of Botany,* visited Fort Colvile in the winter of 1843–44 to study the vegetation of the region, and in 1843–44 Joseph Burke, a gardener from Kew, spent time at York Factory and in the Saskatchewan and Columbia districts, collecting specimens for the Royal Botanic Gardens.[7]

Such exposure to scientific activity persuaded a few Hudson's Bay Company employees to take up collecting for and corresponding with metropolitan scientists by the 1840s. The efforts of Chief Factors George Barnston and Archibald McDonald, for example, antedated those of the Mackenzie River collectors. Their activities were, however, similarly precipitated by scientific visitors.[8] Even Simpson had a certain weakness for scientific collecting, as evidenced by the museum at his Lachine residence, where he stored curiosities that his employees and others had collected in Rupert's Land and elsewhere.[9]

The company also provided personnel and provisions to expeditions dispatched by the British Crown after 1818 in search of the Northwest Passage; Frederick Beechey, John Franklin, and John Ross and William Parry all benefited from the labor and expertise of Hudson's Bay Company men and native peoples.[10] When British expeditions went missing, the HBC not only directed all of its officers to assist search and rescue missions by providing goods and men but also sponsored three expeditions to search for the Franklin expedition lost in 1845. The 192 Arctic Medals presented by the British Admiralty to HBC employees for services rendered in searching for the Northwest Passage and the missing Franklin expedition recognized their efforts.[11]

In 1859 Simpson agreed to Joseph Henry's request for permission to conduct scientific studies in the Hudson's Bay Company territories and offered to facilitate those studies as much as possible. Kennicott went north armed with a letter of introduction from Simpson and a Smithsonian circular, approved by Simpson and addressed to HBC employees as "friends of science." The circular outlined Smithsonian specimen needs, and Simpson's letter was intended to "secure to Mr. Kennicott a friendly welcome and personal attention" at HBC posts.[12] The documents ensured that William Mactavish, the governor of Assiniboia, and company officers stationed throughout Rupert's Land would assist Kennicott when he arrived at their posts.

The hospitality, fraternity, and cooperation Kennicott met with at posts scattered throughout the Mackenzie River District were thus, in large part, due to Simpson's interest and support. But less altruistic motives also facilitated data collection. Ambitious men, eager to make their mark, were sometimes willing to subvert company policy and were always willing to entice or coerce fellow northerners to work on behalf of the Smithsonian—or, stated more accurately, such aggressive collectors were eager to convince, cajole, or bully others less interested in science to help them fulfill their desires for recognition and prestige within the scientific community.

Corporate cooperation and the initiatives of northern inhabitants therefore ameliorated the limited financial resources available for Kennicott's expedition. Although Baird raised $2,000 to finance Kennicott's expedition, the funds were supposed to pay for everything from Kennicott's travel to gifts for collectors, preservatives, and the costs of shipping specimens between Washington and the Mackenzie River District.[13] Kennicott's expedition differed from earlier government-sponsored expeditions in that it was funded philanthropically and consequently less generously, although neither the mandate nor the practical difficulties of his expedition were any less daunting than those of the many government-funded expeditions sent afield during the first half of the nineteenth century.[14] The geographical impediments of conducting fieldwork far away from the institutional framework of the Smithsonian were certainly no less serious than those found on other expeditions. Five thousand miles separated Fort Yukon from

Smithsonian scientists, and specimens collected in the northern breeding grounds had to be shipped safely and securely by dogsled and canoe, Red River cart, and train for periods of 10 to 13 months.[15] Although it was not apparent until Kennicott returned north in 1865 with the Western Union Telegraph Expedition, Hudson's Bay Company assistance was invaluable to the success of Kennicott's first northern expedition.[16]

Kennicott had some idea of the problems of northern travel through reading exploration narratives, but he was not put off by the obstacles before him when he left Chicago in April 1859. He perhaps should have been intimidated by the distances and terrain, though. Communications and transportation between the Mackenzie River District and Fort Garry, the southernmost post in the HBC territories, were regular but infrequent. Additionally, the 1,500-mile journey to Fort Simpson and beyond was made by canoe, often on rough water, and included long portages and dangerous crossings on large lakes.

Kennicott went north on a fleet of canoes manned by the métis boatmen of the Portage La Loche Brigade. They paddled along the rivers and lakes, passing through Norway House and Cumberland House, and arrived at Methye Portage almost two months after leaving home. Kennicott left the Portage La Loche Brigade at Methye Portage, one of the most grueling portages in Rupert's Land and notable because it was a long, sandy stretch over the height of land between the Churchill and Athabasca rivers. There he joined the canoes of the Mackenzie River Brigade, which transported furs and trade goods between Methye Portage and the northern trading depot. They paddled for more than a month before reaching Fort Simpson. In August 1859, four months after leaving home, the young naturalist from Illinois found himself— along with the 300 pounds of apparatus and supplies that he had brought for collecting natural history specimens—at a remote post in the far north.

The determination and stamina Kennicott exhibited in traveling north were ostensibly out of character in an individual who was in poor health.[17] Kennicott's mother, Mary, always feared for her son's physical and mental well-being. As a youth, Kennicott was believed to have had too delicate a constitution for formal schooling, and at some point in the latter 1840s he contracted malaria.[18] But Kennicott was nevertheless as well trained as most antebellum field naturalists.

Before the Civil War, the most successful scientists and naturalists received their scientific education informally. Despite his ill health, the education Kennicott received was much like that of his contemporaries who obtained scientific instruction surreptitiously through medical colleges or through an apprenticeship with a practicing naturalist.[19] Kennicott received both scientific instruction and encouragement from his father, Dr. John Kennicott, an avid horticulturalist and a physician, and he attended medical school at his mother's insistence. John Kennicott was opposed to any idea of Robert's becoming a physician, favoring instead a career as a naturalist. He promoted that choice by publishing one of his son's natural history articles in the *Transactions of the Illinois State Agricultural Society* and by persuading his colleagues to instruct Robert. John Kennicott was determined that Robert would be a naturalist: "[A] naturalist and nothing else he *will* be—come what may."[20]

Robert acquired some training in physiology from Dr. D. Brainard of Rush Medical College in Chicago. He assisted in Brainard's herpetological research, with the results of their experiments on rattlesnake venom being published in the Smithsonian's *Annual Report* (1854). He also received instruction in ornithology from a highly regarded amateur ornithologist, Dr. Philo Romayne Hoy of Racine, Wisconsin, and he studied natural history under Dr. J. P. Kirtland, the founder of Cleveland Medical College (Western Reserve). An amateur malacologist, Kirtland was ultimately responsible for Kennicott's interest in the north.[21] Kirtland suggested that Russian America, as well as the Hudson's Bay Company territories, would hold unsurpassed potential for natural history studies, and he insisted that Kennicott read Captain Cook's *Voyage to the Pacific Ocean* and George Simpson's *Overland Journey Round the World* to familiarize himself with what little was known of the geography and natural history of the far north.[22]

Kennicott had also acquired experience in the field and was in the process of establishing a reputation as a field naturalist in the decade preceding his Mackenzie River expedition. Chronic illness

View of the Smithsonian Institution, at left in background, before the fire of 1865. (Smithsonian Institution photo 1863)

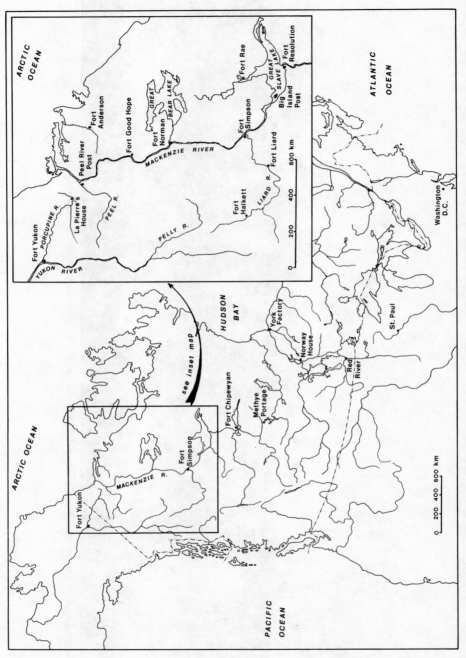

Northern North America, with inset of the Mackenzie River–Smithsonian collecting network. (Map by Victor Lytwyn, University of Manitoba)

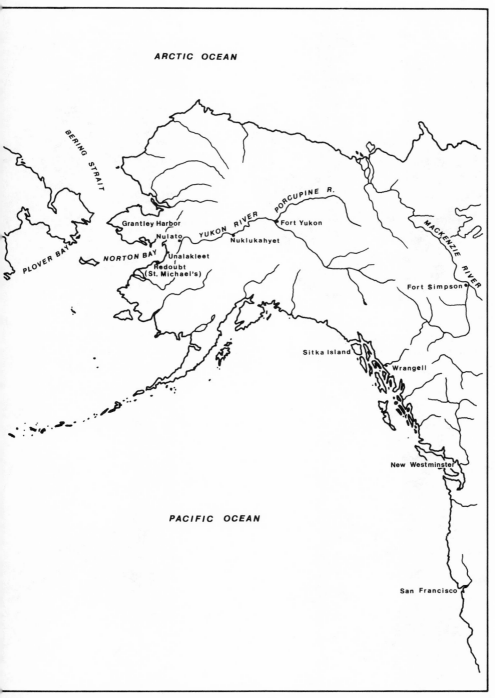

ARCTIC OCEAN

BERING STRAIT

PLOVER BAY

Grantley Harbor

NORTON BAY

Nulato

Unalakleet

Redoubt
(St. Michael's)

YUKON RIVER

Nuklukahyet

PORCUPINE R.

Fort Yukon

MACKENZIE RIVER

Fort Simpson

Sitka Island

Wrangell

New Westminster

PACIFIC OCEAN

San Francisco

Russian America. (Map by Victor Lytwyn, University of Manitoba)

Left, Spencer Fullerton Baird (1823–1887) circa 1860; *right*, Bernard Rogan Ross (1827–1874) circa the 1860s. (Baird, Smithsonian Institution photo 64750; Ross, courtesy of Hudson's Bay Company Archives, Provincial Archives of Manitoba)

Left, James Lockhart (b. ca. 1828) in 1867; *right*, Roderick Ross MacFarlane (1833–1920) in 1870. (Courtesy of Hudson's Bay Company Archives, Provincial Archives of Manitoba)

Robert Kennicott (1835–1866), posing for a studio photograph after his return from the north. Smithsonian Institution photo 43604)

Back view of Fort Simpson, Mackenzie River District, 1852. (Courtesy of Hudson's Bay Company Archives, Provincial Archives of Manitoba)

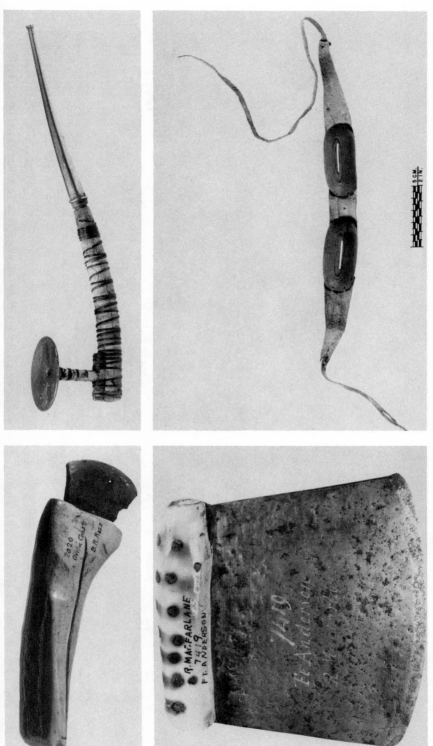

Top left, Inuit scraper sent to the Smithsonian by B. R. Ross; *top right*, "Eskimo" pipe collected by R. R. MacFarlane while he was stationed at Fort Anderson; *bottom left*, meat chopper made by the Inuit trading at Fort Anderson and received by the Smithsonian in January 1869; *bottom right*, snow goggles collected by MacFarlane and received by the Smithsonian in 1866. (Catalogue #2020, #7447, #7449, and #1147, Department of Anthropology, National Museum of Natural History, Smithsonian Institution)

Western Union in Russian America. (From Frederick Whymper, *Travel and Adventure in the Territory of Alaska* [New York: Harper and Bros., 1869])

did not prevent him from sending specimens to the Smithsonian in 1853 and 1854. Nor did his health deter him from undertaking fieldwork on behalf of the Illinois State Agricultural Society. Because the Smithsonian Institution provided financial assistance for the collections made by the Illinois society in 1855, many of Kennicott's specimens were subsequently forwarded to Baird, although they had been collected for the society's exhibit at the Chicago Agricultural Fair.[23]

The importance of Kennicott's Illinois specimens extended well beyond the empirical sphere. Collecting the specimens was one of several events that facilitated the development of a more personal connection between Kennicott and Baird, eventually making Kennicott an "intimate in the Baird family." The two men had been corresponding at least since 1853, they met in Washington in 1854, and in December 1857 Kennicott went to Washington to study with Baird.[24] Collecting for the Illinois society also tested Kennicott's ability to recruit and train lay collectors. The Illinois Central Railroad agreed to cooperate with the society's Smithsonian-funded expedition, and Kennicott was directed "to travel throughout Illinois, especially along the lines of the Illinois Central railroad, and not only to make collections himself, but to instruct the employees of the railroad company and others, so as to enable them to assist in the work."[25] His expedition was a great success, and two years later Kennicott was hired to collect specimens for a new natural history museum at Northwestern University in Evanston, Illinois.

In 1857 Kennicott collected throughout Illinois and as far north as the Red River Settlement, on behalf of Northwestern University. While at Red River, he met several important community leaders. Two of them, Donald Gunn and William Mactavish, played important roles in collecting and transmitting the specimens sent from Rupert's Land to the Smithsonian between 1859 and 1868. During the four months that Kennicott stayed in Red River in 1857, the two men may have convinced him that Hudson's Bay Company employees could be recruited to collect for the Smithsonian.[26] Gunn, for example, had himself been convinced of the importance of Smithsonian science and had been submitting natural history specimens and meteorological registers for at least two years before

Kennicott's visit.[27] Kennicott's successful venture with the Illinois Central Railroad also implied that a collecting program based on volunteer labor might be replicated farther north.

Within 18 months of Kennicott's first visit to Red River, he was on his way to the far Northwest via the Mackenzie River District. Several factors converged to make such a trip not only feasible but also necessary. The enigmatic mixture of ideas and events that launched Kennicott's expedition to arctic America included information about the north and northern zoology obtained on Kennicott's first trip to Red River, Kirtland's conviction that Russian America and Rupert's Land offered unprecedented opportunities for zoological collecting, Baird's desire to acquire the most comprehensive series of North American natural history specimens yet assembled, and the allure of personal testimonials from northern explorers such as Dr. Elisha Kent Kane and Dr. John Rae.[28] Kennicott proposed that he should be the person to go north and gather specimens for the Smithsonian, and Baird agreed enthusiastically.[29]

When Kennicott went to arctic America in 1859, he had scholarly and practical credentials, as well as useful connections with North American scientists. He had been educated by some of the best-known and most reputable amateur naturalists of his day and had proved his abilities as a fieldworker and a descriptive taxonomist. He had written articles on North American herpetology, focusing on collections in Illinois and Washington, and describing some of the snakes collected by the United States and Mexican Boundary Survey and the Pacific Railroad Survey expeditions.[30] An article entitled "The Quadrupeds of Illinois, Injurious or Beneficial to the Farmer," which contained descriptions of the mammals Kennicott had collected between 1855 and 1858, was received favorably by American scientists.[31] While still a young man, Kennicott had accomplished much. By 1859 Kennicott was more than just an anonymous but zealous supporter of the natural sciences. He had been offered the curatorship of Northwestern University's natural history museum; he was on his way to becoming an important member of the North American scientific community.

Although Kennicott's training and expertise were essential to success in the field, his connections with the scientific community and his commitment to science were assets of inestimable worth in the north. In many cases Kennicott provided northerners with their first real contact with the world of science. He acted as an intermediary between isolated Hudson's Bay Company traders and metropolitan scientists and was a role model for would-be collectors. Laurence Clarke, easily one of the most peripatetic collectors of the group, recognized Kennicott's role in motivating him to collect:[32] "A further acquaintance with Mr Kennicott, who's zeal in the pursuit of science cannot be too much applauded, admiration for his many estimable qualities, regard for his amiable character, and a consequent wish to aid him in furthering the objects of his journey to the far North, made me this year take a more lively interest in gathering for [the Smithsonian] Institution."[33]

Kennicott's passionate commitment to the study of natural history was obvious. Endless hours spent in makeshift laboratories, and in the field, proved his sincerity and assured northerners that collecting was important. Moreover, he received no salary, and because he was not independently wealthy, he was not free from financial worry.[34] Although he had barely enough money to purchase the goods he needed from company stores, he persevered without complaint. The unaffected nature of Kennicott's devotion to science was undeniably inspiring, and a strong correlation exists between Kennicott's whereabouts and the years in which most Hudson's Bay Company men sent specimens to the Smithsonian. Approximately four times as many collectors sent specimens in 1860, 1861, and 1862—when Kennicott was traveling throughout the north—as in the five years following his departure.[35] The efforts of many HBC men were due almost entirely to Kennicott's presence.

Northerners were immediately attracted to the mysterious "Bugs" Kennicott. Chief Factor George Barnston, a 40-year veteran of the fur trade and one of the first HBC men whom Kennicott encountered on his way north in 1859, expressed great interest in Kennicott's expedition.[36] Not only was Barnston one of the most senior and influential employees of the Hudson's Bay Company, but he was also well grounded in natural history and colonial science. A prolific contributor to the *Canadian Naturalist and Geologist* and an active member of the Natural History Society of Montreal, he was an avid botanist, entomologist, and ornithologist.[37] He had already deposited natural history specimens with the British Museum, McGill University, the Royal Industrial Museum of Scotland, and the Canadian Geological Museum. Although powerful and worldly in his own way, Barnston had not even heard of the Smithsonian Institution before meeting Kennicott; he did, however, agree to collect specimens.[38] He also offered to ask his friends and co-workers to collect for the Smithsonian.

The two men parted company in Fort William after having traveled by steamer from Collingwood. Kennicott pushed on to Norway House, where he met with HBC governor George Simpson, the company's chief executive officer in Rupert's Land. Although he was always referred to as governor, Simpson was only the overseas governor and was responsible to a governor and directors in London for fur trade operations in North America. Simpson was best known for his business acumen and for his authoritarian and intrusive style of management, but he was also a collector of exotic zoological and ethnological curiosities.[39] He too was interested in the American expedition, and his interest translated into tangible benefits. Simpson offered Kennicott the services of Hudson's Bay Company posts and personnel and granted Kennicott free board and lodgings while at the posts.[40] Only the expenses of Kennicott's personal outfit, including the costs of transportation and freight, as well as salaries for hired help, were excluded from Simpson's offer.[41]

Kennicott soon came to appreciate Simpson's magnanimity. Goods, including provisions, were procured only at great expense in the Mackenzie River District, and Kennicott noted that the Hudson's Bay Company saved him his greatest expense by assuming the cost of his provisions, which was equal to that of a clerk's allowance of £25.[42] But Simpson was completely unwilling to defray transportation or shipping costs, as George Barnston had done. Barnston had given Kennicott free passage and allowed him to take his dog, a traveling companion, and 300 pounds of baggage to Norway House without charge.[43] The governor would not permit the same arrangement for the voyage from Norway House to Fort Simpson; Governor Simpson refused to contravene com-

pany rules and regulations in order to expedite Kennicott's journey to the Mackenzie River District.[44]

Because Kennicott traveled north on the boats that took in the
next year's supply of trade goods and provisions before returning
to Norway House with the furs that had been acquired during the
previous season, his arrival was followed by a flurry of activity.
Sorting and labeling, packing and unpacking, restocking the store,
and auditing inventory and accounts, as well as preparing outgo-
ing correspondence, preoccupied HBC employees after he disem-
barked. Kennicott had arrived at Fort Simpson at one of the
busiest times of the year, but his first impression of the nature of
life at a fur trade post was modified significantly after living at Fort
Simpson for a few months. By mid-November, he had adjusted to
life in the "laziest community" he had ever encountered:

> We breakfast (now) at 8 or 9 o.c. and have dinner at 4. Card
> playing, until we began writing for the packet, has been the regular
> employment in the evening. Though hereafter I mean to insist on
> being permitted to write at least part of the time. The officers duty
> is almost nothing beyond his actual presence. A little less than two
> months in the year is sufficient for all the writing. [N]o wonder
> then they become lazy—Mr Ross and Brother Tadger are the only
> industrious men I've seen here.[45]

Although Fort Simpson was the hub of the Mackenzie River
trade, the usual routine was monotonous and unchanging. Bernard Rogan Ross, the well-educated Protestant Irishman in charge
of Fort Simpson, particularly deplored the lassitude of northern
life.[46] He constantly attempted to alleviate the dullness he associated with life in the fur trade by filling his leisure hours with
activities that were intellectually stimulating, as well as entertaining. Ross fancied himself an accomplished vocalist, and he tried
his hand at poetry and journalism.[47] He loved to read history,
philosophy, poetry, novels, and biographies. In addition to his
personal library of 500 volumes, he had access, after 1852, to the
Mackenzie River District Library and the Officers' Proprietary
Library. By 1859 Ross had also established contact with the
Smithsonian.

Ross's first link to the Smithsonian was probably initiated through his acquaintance with George Gibbs, who became one of Baird's scientific collaborators during the 1860s.[48] Ross had met Gibbs in 1857 when Gibbs was serving as geologist and botanist on the North West Boundary Survey Commission. A New York lawyer who was more interested in science and adventure than in the law, Gibbs went to the West Coast following the discovery of gold.[49] He lived in the Northwest for 12 years, and when he returned east, he was appointed secretary to the Hudson's Bay Claims Commission. His interest and expertise in ethnology and philology made him indispensable to the Smithsonian Institution. Ross and other northerners collected ethnographic data when requested by Gibbs during the 1850s or by the Smithsonian during the 1860s.

Despite Ross's relationship with Gibbs, the northern trader became preoccupied with collecting only after meeting Kennicott. Ross was most eager to assist the naturalist in other ways as well. Kennicott wrote to Baird: "Mr Ross says he will send me and necessary baggage any where in the district from Slave Lake to the Yukon by the regular brigades free gratis for nothing and that if I choose it shall cost me nothing but what I pay for clothes while I stay in his district!!"[50] Although Ross was not quite as generous as he led his visitor to believe, he did take certain risks on the American's behalf. Ross was not in a position to offer free lodging, transportation, or freight to Kennicott, but he did. Such concessions required the consent of the governor and all of the chief traders and chief factors, who together made decisions affecting the fur trade in Rupert's Land; those men had already stipulated that Kennicott was to receive free room and board at Hudson's Bay Company posts but nothing more.[51] Moreover, when Ross suggested that the Smithsonian ship goods into the district in his name, he was deliberately ignoring Simpson's orders. Because the Americans were already burdened with charges for transporting specimens and supplies between Washington and Portage La Loche, Ross suggested that additional costs could be avoided if supplies were sent to him as the officer in charge.[52] Free freight was one of the prerogatives of his position, and Ross chose a liberal interpretation of that privilege. Whereas Barnston stretched company policy a little in Kennicott's favor, liberties taken by Ross made both Barnston and Simpson appear meanspirited.

Simpson's decisions regarding HBC support of Smithsonian science were completely undermined by Ross but not without long-term consequences. Ross's abuses of Hudson's Bay Company facilities and funds not only resulted in some personal cost and embarrassment but also eventually undermined the Smithsonian's appeal to northern collectors. Laurence Clarke wrote to Kennicott regarding Ross's indiscretions: "Barney has done incalculable damage by his dishonest dealings in "K"[. It] was brot home to him of having misappropriated much of the companys property in obtaining his collections, and has been fined heavily by minutes of council this year; the result is, that people on this side feel an atipathy [*sic*] to meddling with collections of any sort."[53] Ross's actions also provoked a reassessment of company support for extra-corporate activities. Following Kennicott's expedition, the company instituted a policy whereby all visitors, scientific or otherwise, had to pay for board and lodgings, and in 1865 Ross's private account with the Hudson's Bay Company was debited £27.6.3 in order to recoup company funds used to finance collecting activities while he was in charge of the Mackenzie River District.[54]

Kennicott knew that Ross had overextended his authority with regard to free freight before the second shipment of specimens left the district in the spring of 1860, but scientific interests seemed to justify collusion.[55] Kennicott also believed that he had to defer to Ross in order to ensure a flow of specimens to the Smithsonian. In letters to Baird, Kennicott often described his efforts to solicit Ross's assistance. The chief trader's help was usually obtained only at great personal sacrifice on Kennicott's part. Ross was one of the most self-indulgent and pompous individuals that Kennicott met during his brief stay in the north. Inordinately conceited, Ross never hid his desire for fame and glory, jumping at every opportunity to claim responsibility for collections and even robbing others of recognition. In 1860 Kennicott wrote Baird:

> I dont know if I ever explained fully that as I found Mr Ross very anxious to send all he could in his own name I agreed that I would teach all I could to Reed and some of the other Postmasters and

clerks who were to hand over to him all the specimens to be sent out in his or his & the collectors names—As I of course wanted to see all the specimens sent possible—I thought this [a] better policy than to have them given to me. The more so as Mr Ross rather insisted on it & agreed to pay any expense. But I find almost all the gentlemen opposed to this, all Ive seen since preferring to give the specimens directly. Clarke says he'll see him d——d first & me too! As he says Mr R. "is too fond of getting others to work and he getting the credit."[56]

Kennicott was seldom negative about any of the collectors whom he had recruited, but he remained civil to Ross only through great self-control. Upon learning that Ross had duped him into thinking that the Hudson's Bay Company collections were procured through his intervention and liberality, Kennicott's reaction was restrained despite inclinations otherwise:

Clarke opened my eyes to the fact of my having been humbugged by Mr Ross. . . . [H]e had given me the meanest kind of a voyaging allowance. Clarke was expressively enraged & would make a row about it if I'd let him—So it seems that Gov Simpson was not forgetting me at all or meaning that I was to live on the gentlemans allowance at whose post I stopped—I am of course hurt that Mr Ross should have treated me so meanly—the more so as he was always recurring [referring?] in my presence to the fact, or rather his statement, that his allowance was short— . . .

You may suppose that after this I shall not think as kindly of some of Mr Ross' disagreeable doings but [I'll] just keep my opinion to myself and play the hypocrite a little—I shall not get into any row with him under any circumstances. . . . I wish I hadnt begun writing about him but as I did begin I've given you an idea of the thing lest you should think I had gotten into some row with him or would be foolish enough to do so,—He doesnt like me more than moderately well but I shall manage to keep him thinking I consider him grand chose—The end sanctions the means[,] the Catholic priest here says.[57]

Kennicott was willing to hide his true feelings about Ross because numerous specimens found their way to the Smithsonian as a result of Ross's efforts. The contributions made by the other Hudson's Bay

Company employees stationed at Fort Simpson paled next to the collections submitted by the duplicitous and rapacious Ross.[58]

Ross's one redeeming feature was his ability to get the job done. Most Hudson's Bay Company collectors were significantly less involved and less committed than Ross. For example, despite weeks of effort, Kennicott could not convince Julian Onion, Fort Simpson's new clerk and one of Kennicott's traveling companions from Norway House, that collecting natural history specimens should be substituted for the card games played during idle hours.[59] Onion and many of his co-workers were unable to see the efficacy of collecting as an escape from the tedium that was a part of life in the north.

Like all clerks, Onion was a man of some education. He was responsible for keeping the written records of the post, including the account books and the "Journal of Daily Occurrences," and his duties demanded a certain aptitude for mathematics and some appreciation of the rigors of science. But though he was a technician of sorts—keeping track of debits and credits, calculating profits and losses, registering daily weather conditions, and recording any information relevant to the trading or provisioning of the post—Onion was not disposed to take part in the technicalities of specimen collection.[60] He submitted less than 1 percent of the specimens sent out from the Mackenzie River District during the 1860s.

Arguments extolling the recreational benefits of collecting were even less successful in converting post supervisors, or postmasters, into fieldworkers.[61] Men such as Thomas Swanston and Andrew Flett had worked for the Hudson's Bay Company for many years as laborers before being promoted to postmasters, who were members of the working class rather than the gentleman class, and more-tangible benefits were needed to sustain enthusiasm for collecting among men from the "servant" class. Kennicott could occasionally cajole such men into collecting by purchasing their assistance with tobacco, alcohol, tea, or sugar, but servants were generally unwilling to persevere as unpaid volunteers.

Although Kennicott was able to recruit almost anyone who took the time to "talk eggs" with him, maintaining the commitment of recruits was more difficult. The boredom and inactivity noted by Ross and Kennicott were rarely experienced by members of the servant class who were responsible for the backbreaking, tedious, and menial tasks at the posts. Servants were responsible for packing and transporting furs, provisions, and trade goods between posts and Indian camps. They were also charged with keeping the icehouse filled, tending crops, securing wood for fuel and lumber, making snowshoes, building sledges, and, above all, tending the fishing nets, which were vital to the sustenance of the posts.[62] It was difficult for the working class to maintain an interest in activities that differed specifically, but not generally, from the many other time-consuming and physically taxing duties assigned them. Servants did not need to resort to collecting in order to fill a void that seldom existed in their workday. Collecting and processing specimens was simply too demanding to hold the interest of employees already engaged in physical labor at the posts. Avian specimens, for example, were acquired only after countless hours of hunting for nests and eggs, crouching in swamps, and tramping over tundra. Those outdoor activities were followed by considerably more hours at skinning, preserving, and packing the specimens destined for the Smithsonian. Hudson's Bay Company servants were accustomed to being paid for similar work and were not inclined to spend their free time working without pay. Such an idea not only was unattractive but also could have established an undesirable precedent.

Most HBC employees made very small contributions. More than 15 "Europeans" were recruited to collect for the Smithsonian during 1860, but their participation was sporadic and unsustained. None of the Fort Simpson laborers contributed more than 2 percent of the total collection sent out of the district. Equally small collections were sent south by servants such as Alexander Mackenzie at Fort Liard, James Dunlop at Fort Halkett, Nicol Taylor at Fort Norman, James Flett at La Pierre's House, and John Reid at Big Island.[63]

Although Chief Trader Bernard Rogan Ross submitted 45 percent of the Mackenzie River specimens received by the Smithsonian in 1860, even officers could be disinclined toward collecting. Kennicott managed to convince W. L. Hardisty, the chief trader in charge at Fort Resolution, and Laurence Clarke, the clerk in charge at Fort Rae, of the importance of his expedition, but the two men submitted few specimens.[64] Hardisty and Clarke both wrote apologetic letters to Baird, blaming their inactivity on occupational demands. Hardisty, for example, wrote:

> I confess that I feel rather humiliated and ashamed of the very inadequate return that I have been able to make in furtherance of your wishes in regard to collections for the Smithsonian Institution.—but the fact is my dear Sir, I have fallen on troublesome times.—opposition to our trade, and the consequent discontent and unsettled state of the Indians arising therefrom, has greatly increased the labours and diffeculties [*sic*] of my position here—and keep me fully employed, especially during the summer months.[65]

Clarke's antipathy toward collecting also reflected an antagonistic relationship with Bernard Rogan Ross. Kennicott alone could persuade Clarke to collect. Clarke objected strongly to Ross's efforts to take all the credit for specimens sent from the Mackenzie River District to the Smithsonian, and his enthusiasm for collecting evaporated when Kennicott left the vicinity of his post at Fort Rae in the spring of 1860.[66]

Kennicott worked out of Fort Simpson only until March 1860. He then moved northwest, arriving at Fort Yukon in December after crossing the Mackenzie Mountain range. Much of the journey had to be made on foot, but Kennicott spared himself at least some of the effort of northern travel by hiring six native people, some of them women, to haul his outfit across the mountains: "[T]he Peel's River 'gals' *are* 'strong' without mistake, for some small *wives* no larger than a southern school girl of ten or twelve years old carried loads of fifty or sixty pounds across the mountains."[67] Northern travel was never easy, but Kennicott had learned from his Hudson's Bay Company acquaintances how to minimize difficulties by hiring native people to do the hard, menial, or dangerous work.

The Yukon men were happy to have Kennicott stay with them, because visitors were even more infrequent at Fort Yukon than at Fort Simpson. Additionally, life farther north was even less hectic than at Fort Simpson. James Lockhart, the 10-year veteran of the fur trade who was in charge at Fort Yukon, referred to life at his post as one of "exile and banishment," where company employees suffered more than "Siberian exiles."[68]

Lockhart welcomed Kennicott warmly and quickly integrated natural history collecting into his regular routine. The two became friends and confidants, discussing politics, especially the politics and philosophy of slavery, and swapping stories about families, friends, and work.[69] Much of their time was devoted to natural history—"talking eggs," as well as collecting and processing specimens—but the Yukon men also amused themselves with lighter fare. Kennicott wrote: "Mr Lockhart sings very well, and plays the violin, flute and accordian [sic] which three instruments he has, while Bras [sic] the postmaster has a jewsharp! We have grand concerts now and again."[70]

Postmaster William Brass and Lockhart's new apprentice clerk, Strachan Jones, were also soon persuaded to collect for the Smithsonian.[71] Jones was a far more productive recruit than Brass, but then Jones was one of the better educated men in the north. He was a graduate of Toronto College and, according to Kennicott, "a gentleman by birth & education and a *brick*—tho' what is called a dry stick."[72] It was Jones's dour personality that made his company less appealing than that of the convivial Lockhart—or that of the unpolished and unlettered Charles Gaudet.

Kennicott and Gaudet became good friends while Kennicott stayed at the French Canadian postmaster's house on Peel River. Gaudet's rough-and-ready lifestyle intrigued Kennicott, who had suffered numerous indispositions.[73] Kennicott truly admired Gaudet, proudly emulating his rugged outdoor existence. Reveling in the hunting, fishing, and trapping, as well as in the long overland trips made on foot or with dogs, Kennicott especially enjoyed shocking family and friends with graphic depictions of the life he had adopted. For example, he vividly described his exotic northern diet in a letter to Baird's adolescent daughter, Lucy:

> We get plenty of moose & deer (Barren ground carabou [sic]) meat and when tis fresh and fat feast famously. We have also plenty of *tea* and each two bags of flour—sometimes our cook regales us with "bangs" which are cakes made by mixing water with flour and frying the batter in moose or deer tallow—Better than mince pies or even oyster patties . . . are "bangs"!—if eaten in the north at

least. Sometimes too we get deer tongues, moose nose and beaver tails! When we go to the mountains hunting deer we have also deers *eyes,* marrow bones and occasionally porcupines—There is no end to our luxuries,—though I fear you *outsiders* with uncultivated tastes would not appreciate them.[74]

Kennicott stayed in the Yukon for more than a year, but when he began his long journey home to the United States in the autumn of 1861, he had fewer specimens to his credit than he had after his first nine months in the Mackenzie River District. Kennicott had become infatuated with "uncivilized" life, attempting to act out the romanticized depictions of frontier life found in contemporary literature and re-created in his letters and journals. His scientific interests were subordinated to the frontier experience in the far north. Unsurprisingly, the productivity of his Yukon acquaintances also reflected his preoccupation with "savagery"; on average, the Yukon collectors were less productive than those living elsewhere in the district. Only Lockhart made a significant contribution to the Smithsonian, although he sent only about half as many specimens as Ross and one-fifth as many as Roderick Ross MacFarlane.

Roderick MacFarlane was the clerk in charge of Fort Anderson, and his collecting activities were legendary in his own lifetime. He became an avid collector, however, only after accidentally meeting up with Kennicott at Fort Good Hope in February 1862.[75] MacFarlane had previously had a casual interest in collecting, but from 1862 to 1865 his collecting activities were incessant. He became consumed with the "oological fever" after Kennicott's stopover, sending the Smithsonian more than 5,000 specimens within a five-year period.

Rumors of MacFarlane's preference for gathering specimens at the expense of company business even reached his superiors.[76] His critics doubted his devotion to duty in light of the amount of time and energy he spent searching for specimens. MacFarlane, however, maintained that his zoological expeditions were accomplished "while the duties of the post were by no means neglected."[77] He also believed, in retrospect, that the intimate knowledge of northern water routes obtained through his many zoological expeditions benefited the Hudson's Bay Company because his data provided information necessary to analyze the feasibility of using steam-powered craft on the Mackenzie River.[78] MacFarlane no doubt overstated the nonzoological value of specimen-collecting expeditions, but he did not overestimate his knowledge of northern geography and river systems. He had done a considerable amount of exploring and surveying in the north— even during his first decade as an HBC employee. He explored the Beghula, or Anderson, River in 1857 and again in 1860, and he established Fort Anderson in 1861 to facilitate trade with the northernmost Inuit.

Compared with Ross, MacFarlane was above reproach in his involvement with the Smithsonian. Even though MacFarlane made four major overland trips to the Arctic Ocean in search of birds and eggs, he was never penalized for any improprieties. Moreover, his relationship with Kennicott, though never intimate, was collegial and trouble-free. Nor did MacFarlane's passion for collecting incite resentment among his co-workers. His industriousness, honesty, and humility were applauded, whereas Ross's thirst for recognition was often derided, as in a letter from W. L. Hardisty to Kennicott: "Mr MacFarlane continues his collections more indefaticably [sic] in order I think to acquire similar honours as those conferred on Mr Ross—with the difference that the latter gained his distinction by the labors of others while MacFarlane's collections are all his own."[79] MacFarlane's collections were his own to the extent that they had been bought and paid for, rather than claimed underhandedly.

Although it is true that, as a clerk, MacFarlane did not have the power or privileges available to an officer like Ross, MacFarlane was as eager as Ross to have others perform the menial, laborious, and unpleasant tasks associated with collecting. Whereas Ross bolstered his own collecting capabilities by tampering with company funds and stealing credit from other collectors, MacFarlane became an expert at using native labor to procure scientific specimens. Indeed, he became dependent on the labor of Athapaskan and Inuit collectors. That dependence became especially obvious in 1866 when many of his "best and most experienced native collectors" succumbed to scarlatina, measles, and influenza. Twenty percent of the Mackenzie River native population died during the winter of 1865–66, and MacFarlane's collection was only one quarter as large as the collections he had sent out during the previous two years. In 1867 a "billious fever" struck an already weakened population, leaving even fewer able-bodied persons capable of collecting.[80] That year MacFarlane submitted only one-quarter the number of specimens sent out in 1866, and all of them were ethnographic. In just two years MacFarlane's collections were reduced to a small fraction of their former size.

Disease had an immediate and deleterious effect on zoological collecting, but it also affected acquisitions indirectly. High mortality rates among the native population meant reduced fur returns. Fort Anderson was therefore abandoned, and MacFarlane was relocated to Fort Simpson. The effects of the move extended well beyond the loss of an experienced coterie of collectors. Although only a clerk, MacFarlane had been the officer in charge at Fort Anderson; he had made the fort a center of scientific operations just as the Hudson's Bay Company had made it the center of the Inuit trade. At Fort Simpson, W. L. Hardisty was in charge; Mac-Farlane was his assistant. In addition, Fort Simpson was just one of many posts in the upper end of the Mackenzie River drainage system, whereas Fort Anderson had been far removed from the other posts in the district. Unlike most HBC posts in the Mackenzie River District, Fort Anderson did not drain into the Mackenzie River system. It had been built just inside the Arctic Circle on the banks of a river that drained directly into the Arctic Ocean. In 1862 when MacFarlane opened up the Anderson, he found himself very isolated, but with considerable autonomy and enormous influence over trade with the native population living to his north and east. In 1866 when he moved south to Fort Simpson, where the economic and social relations between natives and non-natives were less limited, he lost his power and influence, as well as his independence. Zoological collections of the magnitude of those submitted by MacFarlane between 1862 and 1865 were made through coercion at least as much as through cooperation, but at Fort Simpson, MacFarlane was not in a position to direct or even to focus native labors. In 1866 MacFarlane discovered what scientists such as Baird already knew: It was virtually impossible to assemble large collections without a large work force.

4

⟨✦⟩

A LABOR OF LOVE, OR JUST PLAIN LABOR?

Experience had taught scientists that long-term residents not only were adept at procuring natural history specimens but also could distinguish between migratory and resident species and provide information on habits and habitat. Despite misgivings about the intellectual capabilities and "superstitious" inclinations of "uncivilized" peoples, scientists believed that even people holding pre-modern or animistic views of the natural world could be employed profitably in the field.

Ornithologists and oologists were certainly aware of the advantages of having a large contingent of indigenous collectors working on their behalf.[1] Although nineteenth-century natural scientists were not particularly interested in the worldviews of a work force that had a "pre-scientific" or "folk" approach to understanding, explaining, and ordering its existence, the English oologist Alfred Newton urged all field naturalists to cultivate and reward native initiatives: "The best allies of the collector are the residents in the country, whether aboriginal or settlers, and with them he should always endeavor to cultivate a close intimacy, which may be assisted by the offer of small rewards for the discovery of nests or eggs."[2] In the Smithsonian's "Instructions for Oological Collecting," Thomas Mayo Brewer agreed with Newton: "The services of boys and other persons on farms, plantations, etc., may be called to great advantage into requisition in collecting eggs."[3]

The collections sent south from the subarctic between 1859 and 1867 certainly represented an effort that far exceeded the capabilities and dedication of the small group of men who received official recognition from American scientists. Ross, MacFarlane, Lockhart, and Kennicott were all acknowledged regularly as important Smithsonian contributors, and they undeniably devoted considerable time and energy to collecting, but so did many others.

In the Mackenzie River District there was a large indigenous population that could supply the labor and the expertise needed to obtain northern specimens, and these people were willing to collect the scientific specimens wanted by the Smithsonian in return for non-native commodities.[4] Many Athapaskans and Inuit already had considerable experience with a socioeconomic system in which European trade goods were exchanged for the products of their labor, and collecting zoological specimens fitted into the existing trade relationship relatively easily. Fieldwork was therefore incorporated into well-established native–fur trade economies; specimens were traded along with furs, fish, and game at Hudson's Bay Company posts.

Scientific specimens became the basis of an exchange system in which the efforts of collectors, like those of hunters and trappers, were traded for goods and salaries. Men, women, and children were all integrated into the expanded trade network. Raisins and sugar were used to persuade youngsters to collect easily accessible specimens, but most native collectors received American consumer items in return for their efforts.[5] Handkerchiefs, silk ribbons and hat cords, jewelry, cotton and calico textiles, calico shirts, feathers, pipe heads, pocketknives, needles, thread, and tobacco formed the majority of the goods exchanged for specimens.[6] Double-barreled guns were occasionally offered to the best collectors, both native and European, as well as other eminently practical items.[7] Collecting apparatus, dissecting kits, microscopes, spyglasses, and pocket compasses, as well as revolvers, felt hats, mosquito nets, dog blankets, dog bells, pipes, opera glasses, and burning glasses, were sent north.[8] Baird also sent gifts to the "country-born" wives and families of some of the northern collectors.[9] The Gaudet,

Reid, Hardisty, James Sibbeston, and William James McLean families received dyes, "crying doll babies," belt buckles, glass necklaces, beads, scissors, silk thread, buttons, hairpins, hairnets, and handkerchiefs.[10]

Although nineteenth-century naturalists were more than willing to exploit native knowledge and energy, they were particularly careful to point out that the "savages" or "half civilized" had intellectual limitations. Considerable skepticism was expressed about the indigenous individual's ability to comprehend scientific matters. Thomas Mayo Brewer, for example, attempted to compensate for such deficiencies by suggesting that native fieldworkers be strictly supervised:

> Whenever they have found a nest, . . . it should not be disturbed before information is communicated to, and the spot visited by some one competent to determine the species, unless the parent can be taken with the nest.

> For eggs not taken by the collector himself, but brought in by natives, or persons not having a scientific knowledge of ornithology, the *local* name or the name applied by the finder *should* only be used, unless indeed it requires interpretation, when the scientific name may be added, but *always within brackets.*[11]

Such precautionary remarks were usually wasted on the nonnative members of the Mackenzie River collecting community. Collectors such as Ross and MacFarlane no doubt believed that Brewer's sanctions referred to native collectors rather than to self-taught scientists such as themselves, but even Ross and MacFarlane were novices. The Mackenzie River collectors were inconsistent and idiosyncratic. They sometimes accepted native identifications but often made their own identifications based on Baird's bird and mammal catalogues.[12] Even when using Baird's guides, however, Ross was often guilty of making "queer identifications" based on "imagination" rather than on fact.[13] His and other erroneous identifications were later corrected by Baird at the Smithsonian.[14]

Despite beliefs in their inherent superiority over native co-workers in scientific matters, Hudson's Bay Company trader-collectors such as Ross and MacFarlane often did not distinguish the work done by themselves personally from that done by native assistants. Ambition and narrow-mindedness meant that aboriginal collectors were seldom acknowledged as recommended. Ross never credited his native assistants with any significant contributions, although he did not hesitate to employ native people to brave the hordes of mosquitoes that plagued the spring breeding grounds.[15] Other collectors also censored accounts of native contributions: Charles Gaudet used native collectors, and in 1864 he regularly employed two individuals in particular; in 1865 Strachan Jones sent an Indian into the Rocky Mountains specifically to collect natural history specimens; James Lockhart hired François Beaulieu to collect eggs at Salt River in 1864 and employed Olivier Laferte as a collector at Fort Rae in the spring of 1865.[16] Lockhart also used local collectors when procuring his Yukon collections, paying them with tobacco and other store goods. Kennicott had given Lockhart five pounds of tea to trade for tobacco, as well as £5 to purchase the items needed to pay for specimens procured by native collectors.[17] The contributions made by these hired field-workers were not formally acknowledged.

Kennicott's first real recruit to his 1859 expedition also employed native assistants to collect natural history specimens.[18] The chief factor of Michipicoten, George Barnston, not only relied on native knowledge of the natural world but also valued it. While most of the Hudson's Bay Company collectors glossed over the role that native expertise played in the acquisition of natural history specimens and data, Barnston acknowledged the contributions and often deferred to native opinion. For example, when his native collectors identified a trout specimen as a distinct variety called the bear trout, or "Macqua," he suggested *Ursina* as an appropriate species name for it.[19] Native collectors supported their differentiation of the "Macqua" species from *Salmo siscowet* (first identified by Louis Agassiz in 1850) on the basis that the two fish had different spawning seasons. Barnston's proposal for a taxonomic revision of lake trout based on native observations did not alter ichthyological classifications, though; all varieties of lake trout are considered to belong to one species. Barnston was somewhat more successful when he proposed revisions to the genus *Lutra*. Barnston accepted the opinion of his native informants regarding distinctions among otters, and he again asked Baird to name one species in honor of the Algonkian word for the animal. Although Barnston rather than Baird was credited with naming *Lutra destructor* as a separate species, his identification was later refuted when *Lutra destructor* was discovered to be synonymous with *Lutra canadensis canadensis*.[20]

Barnston's view of native expertise and competency in the field was shared by Donald Gunn, a Red River settler who consistently purchased nests and eggs from indigenous collectors throughout the more than 10 years that he collected for the Smithsonian.[21] In 1857 he sent Baird specimens that had been collected, skinned, and stuffed by aboriginal people. The next year, Gunn promised Baird that he would request the "Indians in my service" to collect eggs in the region of Lake Winnipeg, and he again referred to buying nests and eggs as well as bribing native people to collect for him. Gunn also employed some native boys for the 1862 and 1864 breeding seasons, and when he went on an egging expedition to Lake Winnipeg in 1866, he depended on native help and expertise: "It is true, I could have gone to the Lakes without an Indian and secured plenty Eggs and some parent birds,—but many sets of these Eggs parentage I could not identify and would on that account be of little or no value—Whereas an Indian on securing an Egg knows at once what kind of bird is its parent.[22] The Smithsonian had provided financial assistance for Gunn's expedition in anticipation of receiving the specimens that would be collected on and around Lake Winnipeg, and Gunn used the money to pay for native help. Each man engaged for the egging trip earned approximately four shillings, while boys earned from one to two shillings.[23]

Gunn's remarks about his native collectors could also be disparaging. He stated that native people were not only unreliable but also uncooperative. They preferred to eat eggs rather than collect them, and he lamented that native collectors were capable of becoming astute negotiators once they were aware of the value of an article.[24] Gunn's contradictory stance was not unusual. European collectors were generally more given to cursing the inadequacies they so readily detected in their native assistants than to praising the assistants' good work.[25] Laurence Clarke and B. R.

Ross, for example, expressed fundamental reservations, questioning the capabilities of native people on the basis that their "superstitious" beliefs prevented them from collecting. Some would-be collectors complained that native people preferred to feign ignorance rather than cooperate, and even MacFarlane attributed errors made in packing his specimens to the "stupidity of Indians."[26] Although MacFarlane used native labor more frequently than any other northern collectors—and acknowledged his dependence regularly—he did not hesitate to attribute any shortcomings in his collections to his assistants.

Kennicott was more forthcoming in his notes on the contributions of native collectors, and he appreciated their knowledge of the natural world to the extent that he recorded names given birds and mammals in the Kutchin and Liard Slavey dialects.[27] But when Kennicott encountered difficulties in arousing native support for his work, he too became exasperated with what he interpreted as restiveness. In 1860 he wrote Baird, deriding the capabilities and initiative of northern native people: "[The Indians are] the most unobliging imaginable and as big rascals as such idiots *can* be. I can scarce get anything from them, and what few specimens I do get I must pay large prices for. So long as an Indian isnt hungry—or in fact *very* hungry—he is as independant [*sic*] as you please and quite scorns the idea of working for anything less than very large pay, if he will work at all."[28] The more that native labor was needed, the dearer it became.

Deprecatory characterizations of native people were so common as to constitute a convention in the Mackenzie River–Smithsonian correspondence. But overt criticisms of native productivity, aptitude, and cooperation were rarely indicative of native capabilities or participation in the collecting process. Even Kennicott's first batch of specimens contained skins that had been prepared by Inuit collectors. When the first Athapaskan and Inuit collectors brought zoological specimens to him in the autumn of 1859, he took the opportunity to teach them how to prepare study skins.[29] Kennicott instructed women and boys, as well as men, to skin and preserve specimens. He showed them how to open a specimen by making an incision from the lower end of the breastbone to the anus, how to remove organs, how to scrape away muscle and fat, and how to apply plaster of paris to absorb blood and grease. He then demonstrated how the wings were to be separated from the skeletal frame, how the brains and eyes were to be removed from the skull, and how arsenic or arsenical soap was to be applied. Once preservative had been applied, the skin was to be pulled back into its normal position, appendages were to be tied into place, stuffing inserted, and the incision stitched. The steps had to be followed systematically and performed carefully, so as to produce a high-quality specimen. This the native assistants did.

Kennicott had great faith in the abilities of native collectors. He viewed Inuit people as especially intelligent, noting that some were able to master the art of skinning natural history specimens after just one lesson. Over the winter of 1859–60 Kennicott took the time to teach one young man in particular. This "small savage," as Kennicott referred to him, became so proficient in specimen preparation that during March, when Bernard Ross went on a collecting binge, the boy was kept "hunting and skinning all the time."[30]

Ross skinned only a fifth of the more than 500 specimens collected between March and June 1860. In the following year the majority of Ross's collection was skinned by William Flett, the "mixed-blood" son of an Orcadian laborer named James Flett. Indeed, Ross was proud to point out that he had supervised the entire operation associated with getting specimens ready for export.[31] He was more interested in coordinating a collections program in that part of the Mackenzie River District under his control than in doing the "mechanical" work that others could be hired to do.[32] He preferred to delegate the menial labor to his "deputy skinners." Ross also liked to devote his efforts to what he perceived as the more scientific work associated with specimen collection. Although he avoided many of the tasks associated with preparing specimens, he regarded the responsibility of measuring and identifying specimens as worthy of his attention. The pages in Ross's specimen invoice are therefore filled with columns of data; measurements of body appendages and notes on the sex and seasonal distribution of hundreds of zoological specimens are recorded alongside the scientific names.[33]

Kennicott similarly avoided skinning whenever possible. The American naturalist lamented his ineptitude in the workroom. He never took less than half an hour to skin even a small specimen, so he entrusted all of the more common species to his native skinners. In 1860 most of Kennicott's ornithological specimens were skinned by an Athapaskan woman: "[I have trained her] to skin birds pretty decently—tho she makes no really good skins—and have her skin those I havent time to do—nearly all of the parents of eggs are her skins."[34] That same spring he taught skinning procedures to the native inhabitants at Big Island, where he again found that one woman "made very decent skins."[35] His faith in their ability to competently skin the majority of his specimens reveals more about native expertise than his halfhearted praise for their work. Native people would not have been employed to prepare specimens unless they were efficient, reliable, and skilled.

Kennicott usually had a native person skinning specimens as he collected them, and he rationalized this division of labor by contending that his skills as a naturalist were better utilized in the field than in the workroom. He also, however, relied on native assistance in the field. He was aided by one "Indian wife," for example, who could unequivocally and correctly identify some rare oological specimens after having sighted the parents.[36] Native labor also facilitated Kennicott's journey to Fort Yukon, and when he arrived there in December 1860, he immediately employed native collectors, instructing them "to bring in porcupines, ermines, mice, shrews, . . . marmots etc etc."[37] In addition, he scouted about for the native assistants required for collecting during the avian breeding season, confident that come spring he would have at least 100 boys hunting nests.[38] By the end of May, Kennicott, James Lockhart, and several native collectors were spending 18 hours a day in the field.

Egg collecting was, Kennicott wrote, "glorious sport," but it was also a process that even experts such as Baird, Brewer, and Newton viewed as intuitive rather than demonstrative. Kennicott's northern journal contains one of the few extant descriptions of oological fieldwork:

> From the last of May till now (June 24th) Lockhart and I have been at work generally about eighteen hours out of every twenty-four. As it is light all night (indeed for a week we see the sun at midnight, by refraction, I suppose), we pay little attention to the

time of day, but just work as long as we can keep awake. We start off from the fort with several Indians and canoes, and go through a series of lakes, making portages between these and the various small rivers (both lakes and rivers are very numerous), thus making a turn of fifty to one hundred miles in two or three days. We always go with at least two canoes and a party of four, and when we enter a lake one of the occupants of one canoe hunt in it through the grass at the edge of the lake where the loons, grebes, and canvas-back ducks nest, while his companion wades in the shallow water among the grass, near shore, where we get *Fulix marila* and *F. affinis* (scaup ducks) eggs, and sometimes a nest of *Dafila acuta* (pin-tail duck), that is near the water, or a canvas-back duck in shoal water. The nests are found by seeing the female rise from them. For widgeon's eggs we hunt through the bushes, and for pin-tail ducks, too, generally. When we find spots that seem to promise good breeding ground ashore, we leave the canoes and hunt through the woods and open, dry spots. We camp during the middle of the day at some good point for collecting, nominally to sleep, but, in fact, we sleep very little. I was at one time out three days, in which time I slept only once, and then scarce six hours, when I had already been forty-eight hours without sleep. I am making up for last winter's hibernation.

The hunting in the canoes is glorious sport, but unfortunately we do not get the best collections in them, but while wading, or on land, in both of which situations the mosquitoes are *horrible* beyond all conception. I often long for a temperature of 50 or 60 below zero that I might be relieved from them. It is not the cold, but the mosquitoe, that is the hardest thing to endure in the north.[39]

The collectors' relentless pace was permitted by the long days that characterize northern summers and by the fortitude of the natives who manned the canoes and waded through swamps, ferreting out water birds and uncovering nests.

Kennicott obtained specimens from several Athapaskan collectors, depending heavily on the cooperation of "Red-Leggins," or Ba-Kich-na-chah-teh, the Black River chief of the Kutch-a-kutch-in of whom Kennicott wrote: "[He has brought me] the best things I have obtained from [the] Indians, but has made his *Chil-a-ques* (young men) collect for me too."[40] But many more specimens could be obtained through contractual arrangements. Soon after arriving at Fort Yukon, Kennicott hired Antoine Hoole, a "half breed" interpreter, to collect specimens. Kennicott quickly discovered that hired help like Hoole guaranteed the best collections. He wrote Baird: "We get very little of value from the Indians, in oology at least, unless they are thus regularly engaged."[41]

According to Chief Trader W. L. Hardisty, Hoole was reliable, intelligent, and capable of learning collecting and preservation techniques. All northerners could claim some expertise at skinning and preparing the skins of fur-bearing animals, but the majority of the specimens sent to the Smithsonian were ornithological and oological, and the skinning and preservation of those specimens differed enough from ordinary skinning procedures to necessitate specific training. Both natives and Europeans had to be taught the procedures for the preparation of scientific study skins, and native collectors not only were capable of learning the procedures but also were almost always more skilled than the Hudson's Bay Company collectors at hunting and preparing zoological specimens. Skins obtained from native collectors were better prepared than those from Strachan Jones, the assistant clerk at Fort Yukon who recognized his limitations and commented on them.[42] They were even better prepared than those of Roderick R. MacFarlane, the Fort Anderson clerk whose donations to the Smithsonian during the 1860s exceeded those of any other private contributor.[43] Although MacFarlane's collections were reputed to be second only to one other individual donation made during the first 50 years of the Natural History Department's existence at the Smithsonian, he characterized many of his own specimens as "indifferently prepared." That indifference was partly due to insufficient supplies, but it was also due to MacFarlane's having "not the least taste for the art of taxidermy."[44] Although aptitude and inclination could reflect individual predispositions, technical expertise could be developed only after instruction and practice. James Lockhart, the clerk at Fort Yukon who befriended Kennicott, regretted his ineptitude at skinning, but he anticipated some improvement in his scientific skills following instruction:

[W]hen I arrived here autumn 1859, I began skinning, or rather attempting to skin birds & beasts—all that came in my way, but after a dozen failures, I gave up in despair and determined that I would do nothing until I could learn how to do it *properly:* for I was then aware that Mr. Kennicott would be wintering here with me, and would put me through, what he calls, "a course of sprouts." This he has very kindly done, and has taken an immense deal of trouble to drive into my thick head and clumsy fingers, the thousand little minutia of collecting generally.[45]

Native collectors were as technically adept as, or more adept than, their European counterparts, but they had other important attributes as well. Hoole, for example, was an interpreter with considerable influence in the native community. Upon meeting him, Kennicott quickly recognized that his linguistic talents and social standing could be used to recruit, organize, and coordinate a contingent of native collectors. Kennicott therefore had Hoole "tell every Indian who comes to the fort to bring certain special desiderata," and through Hoole he was able to train a "savage taxidermist" and three "savage collectors."

Hoole and his trainees were indispensable to Kennicott's expedition. Any qualms Kennicott might have had about their alleged primitiveness were repressed. Indeed, Hoole's value to northern science was sufficiently great to provoke Kennicott into remarking upon it and to justify extravagant gifts in return for his services:

Antoine Hoole the interpreter of the post is as I have said a very keen hunter and takes kindly to the collecting, in which I have gotten him thoroughly interested; and he declares there shall be a very loud cry of bereavement among the parents of rare eggs every spring hereafter throughout this region. I consider his work and interest with the Indians a matter of prime importance to arctic zoological operations. I have bribed him with many very acceptable presents and shall give some of the things sent from The Grove for my own use—That *accordian* [*sic*] you sent he has been very anxious to get,—as he will. I have promised him that so long as he will collect for the gentleman in charge here I'll send him annually from the States after my return things which he is highly delighted in the expectation of.[46]

Well aware of the importance of his new position, Hoole instructed others with relish: "The Indians too will then know what is wanted; and I shall not let any of them leave the fort this summer without receiving a long lecture from Antoine upon the immense importance to science of Lockhart's receiving 5000 eggs of wax wing, Picoides, swan, Hawk owl & the like."[47]

Although persuading Hoole to head up fieldwork in the Yukon was essential to the success of Kennicott's expedition, collections made by the Athapaskans and Inuit who traded at Fort Anderson were instrumental to MacFarlane's efforts for the Smithsonian. When Kennicott stayed at Good Hope in 1862, he not only "talked eggs" with MacFarlane but also taught some of the native people living near the fort how to prepare scientific specimens, and he provided MacFarlane with the information needed to recruit his own contingent of native collectors.[48] After spending six weeks with Kennicott at Good Hope, MacFarlane returned to Fort Anderson just in time for the "egging season" and immediately sought out native persons to collect for him.[49] Three weeks later, on 19 June, he left Fort Anderson with five assistants on a 17-day overland egging expedition to Franklin Bay on the Arctic Ocean.

Between 1862 and 1865 MacFarlane made four important expeditions to the arctic coast, and he was always accompanied by native persons whose expertise in zoological identification and habitats was crucial to the success of the trips. On more than one occasion his native assistants even risked life and limb to obtain specimens. In one letter to Baird, MacFarlane provided a vivid account of the perils encountered in collecting a clutch of golden eagle eggs that were perched 30 feet from the summit of the face of a 60-to-70-foot embankment. One of the young men climbed up the cliff, removed the eggs, brought them for examination, and then returned them to the nest in hopes that the mother would reappear. MacFarlane and his crew waited three hours before abandoning their watch without having seen the mother. On their return from the arctic coast, they checked the nest, but the mother had vanished. They had therefore spent several hours simply attempting to verify their preliminary identification of the eggs through corroboration with an adult specimen.

The same exercise was repeated in the same spot the following year,[50] and if similar efforts were devoted to collecting all, or even some, of the specimens, then the amount of time invested by northern collectors was substantial. Inexperience was undoubtedly an important factor in initially prolonging the collecting process, but collecting and preparing specimens were exacting and labor-intensive activities. They were also tedious and sometimes dangerous. Although a great deal of that time, effort, and risk represented native time, effort, and risk, MacFarlane promised "great" collections from his post. Expertise could, MacFarlane assured Baird, be developed through instruction and experience.[51] He was sure that once "his Indians" were made aware of the Smithsonian's needs and had become proficient in the capture and preparation of specimens, they would be prodigious collectors.

MacFarlane dispatched Athapaskan and Inuit collectors "at every opportunity," obtaining an inestimable number of zoological specimens from native fieldworkers.[52] The quantity of ethnological artifacts MacFarlane obtained from native peoples is easier to determine, however. All of them came from his native trading partners. Indigenous cultural artifacts had always had an economic value, but their value as salable items in the native–non-native scientific trading network emerged in the Mackenzie River District in the late 1860s. During those years, native artifacts were becoming one of the most eagerly sought-after northern commodities; when native people were willing to part with objects of their material culture, they received compensation analogous to that given for zoological specimens. The Inuit trading at Fort Anderson sold MacFarlane more than 500 anthropological artifacts, or 50 percent of the entire ethnographic collection sent out of the north during the 1860s. Moreover, almost 50 percent of the entire Mackenzie River anthropological collection was sent south in just one year: More than 480 individual entries, some representing multiple or duplicate specimens of native manufactures, were recorded in the Smithsonian accession registers for 1866. In that year the Mackenzie River native population was suffering the worst effects of scarlatina, measles, and influenza. When northern natives became too incapacitated to hunt, they could trade their weapons, tools, household effects, and other personal possessions for provisions and merchandise from the company store. Many did.

5

⟨⦾⟩

NORTHERN COLLECTORS AND ARCTIC ANTHROPOLOGY

"Antiquities" and ethnographic "curiosities" could be found in European museums such as the Louvre, the Rijksmuseum voor Volkenkunde (Leiden), the British Museum, and the Peter the Great Museum of Anthropology and Ethnography in Leningrad, but the specimens sent by northern traders and trappers to the Smithsonian Institution between 1861 and 1871 were among the first anthropological artifacts received by a North American scientific institution.[1] Archaeology and ethnology were not priorities at the Smithsonian—or in North America generally—before 1860, although the Smithsonian had received a small number of Indian "curiosities" with the Patent Office collection in 1857, including an "Indian Pillow," a "Blanket made of feathers by the natives of California," some "Wooden masks carved by the natives of the north west coast of America," and a few poorly identified technological and decorative items collected by government expeditions sent west.[2] When Kennicott discovered, however, that two Scotsmen had received ethnological specimens from Rupert's Land, he was motivated to collect indigenous artifacts. Because George Wilson of the Royal Scottish Museum and Andrew Murray of Edinburgh had already obtained the support of northern traders in the formation of their anthropological collections, Kennicott asked

Baird: "Are Indian dresses and implements wanted? That is, I mean, shall I get any large number. . . . I suppose for some museums such thing[s] would be desirable[.] I'm getting a few things of the kind."[3] Although Kennicott was sent north in search of zoological specimens, he immediately recognized that the Smithsonian might want to collect "Indian" and "Esquimaux" peculiarities."

Kennicott was right. The Smithsonian was not to be outdone. In 1861, while he was still traveling through the north, the Smithsonian published and distributed its first directions in aid of anthropological collections. "Instructions for Archaeological Investigations in the U. States" (1861) and the later "Instructions for Research Relative to the Ethnology and Philology of America" (1863) were written by George Gibbs, the Smithsonian's first linguist and collaborator on ethnology and philology.[4] Gibbs's instructions were designed to correct collecting habits that, for example, relegated specimens received from the Patent Office to nonscientific purposes. They were also, of course, intended to facilitate acquisitions.

The few artifacts that had been collected by government exploring expeditions were little more than novelties. Carelessly and inadequately identified, they had usually been submitted without notes on tribal origin or specific function.[5] By channeling collecting activities toward specific goals, Gibbs's instructions were supposed to prevent future anthropological collections from replicating the deplorable situation found among the Patent Office specimens. The guides were comprehensive, providing practical suggestions: "In making these [anthropological] collections care should be taken to specify the tribes from whom they are obtained, and where any doubt may exist, the particular use to which each is applied."[6]

Gibbs's instructions dealt with the subjects deemed relevant by archaeologists and ethnologists living in a period dominated by the ethos of racism and evolution. The guides reflected a belief that aboriginal cultures were pristine and unchanging, although primitive. By 1860, North American scientists had accepted the tripartite delineation that European scientists had devised to explain the development of Old World prehistory. Examples of stone, bronze, and iron manufactures were integral to the verification of a theory that associated societal development with technological advance.[7] The antiquities to be obtained through archaeological excavations were therefore valued additions to the Smithsonian collections.[8] Archaeology allowed access to archaic technologies, and Gibbs described the contents of shell beds, the human remains, the weapons, and the implements that could depict the development of extinct societies. He pointed out that the relics and paleontological specimens that were collected according to his instructions would fall "naturally" within the chronological periods identified by stone, bronze, and iron technology.[9]

But Gibbs also proposed a supplementary periodization for pre-contact North America. Moreover, he integrated the westward diffusion of European culture within the technological divisions. Archaic society had already begun to disappear before the arrival of Europeans, but Gibbs believed that contact had compressed the last two stages of North American "prehistory" within a mere 400-year period. Living aboriginal Americans therefore represented the final stage of prehistoric development. Contact had allegedly accelerated the "inevitable" demise of Stone and Bronze Age societies and had supposedly transformed existing Amerindian societies irrevocably. The value of native artifacts was therefore enhanced by the belief that the opportunity to collect them would be short-lived. Native societies were thought to be disappearing, or at the very least "exchanging their own manufactures for those of the white races." Gibbs particularly suggested the collection of

> dresses and ornaments, bowes and arrows, lances, war-clubs, knives, and weapons of all kinds, saddles with their furniture, models of lodges, parflesh packing covers and bags, cradles, mats, baskets of all sorts, gambling implements, models of canoes (as nearly as possible in their true proportions), paddles, fish-hooks and nets, fish-spears and gigs, pottery, pipes, the carvings in wood and stone of the Pacific coast Indians, and the wax and clay models of those of Mexico, tools used in dressing skins and in other manufactures, metates or stone mortars, &c., &c.[10]

Anthropological collections would ensure, in the absence of living Amerindian societies, access to a heritage possibly denied future

CHAPTER 5

scholars. Collecting became a priority for people like Gibbs who were convinced that native societies would at best be assimilated but would more probably be annihilated. The Smithsonian's anthropological instructions therefore combined several interests: the relatively new preoccupation with technological factors as indexes of societal development, a lingering fascination for racial distinctiveness, and the desire to preserve any and all of Amerindian material culture.[11] Curatorial acquisitiveness was, it seemed, eminently justifiable on scientific grounds.

Baird asserted as early as 1863 that the Smithsonian's northern anthropological collections were unequaled: "It is believed that no such series is elsewhere to be found of the dresses, weapons, implements, utensils, instruments of war and of the chase, &c., &c., of the aborigines of Northern America."[12] It was certainly true that anthropological specimens collected in the north arrived in Washington in far greater numbers than any previous donations had, but by the end of 1863 the Smithsonian had received only 146 anthropological specimens from the Mackenzie River District.[13] The contribution was impressive, but it represented only 13 percent of the total collection received from Hudson's Bay Company employees in more than a decade of active collecting.

The Institution received hundreds of anthropological "peculiarities" that had been either collected or constructed by northern traders and trappers. Athapaskan and Inuit craftsmen and craftswomen made models of snowshoes, canoes, kayaks, bows, quivers, arrows, spears, sledges, lodges, and even clothing.[14] The Inuit collections were particularly comprehensive, but numerous specimens from the Chipewyan, Yellowknife, Kutchin, Dogrib, Slave, Hare, and Nehanny tribes were also submitted. Everything from deerskin lodges to the medicine bones of a medicine man was shipped to Washington.[15] Technological artifacts and articles of native dress were preferred, and specimens of hunting apparatus were well represented in the Mackenzie River collections. Northerners submitted quivers, bows, arrows, snares, spears, and darts, as well as fishing line, tackle, hooks, and nets. Bow-making and carving tools, knives, saws, axes, hatchets, earth chisels, ice picks and scoops, needles, fire bags, and fire drills were also sent. Baskets, buckets, and boxes made of birch bark, grass, and wood were collected. Many pieces of native clothing, including examples of summer and winter apparel worn by northern men, women, and children, were sent to the Smithsonian. Moccasins, shoes, and gloves, particularly if made from exotic furs or skins such as polar bear, seal, or wolverine, accompanied the clothing. Collectors also sent the ceremonial headdress and clothing bestowed on a chief, as well as many other adornments, including copper bracelets and ornaments; purses and belts decorated with ivory, embroidery, quillwork, or beadwork; ivory combs; and wooden snow goggles.

The northern specimens were certainly part of Baird's dream to build the biggest, the best, and the first collection of North American indigenous cultural artifacts, but display criteria were not determining factors in the composition of northern collections. Arctic artifacts were collected almost 20 years before a permanent public display of anthropological specimens was arranged.[16] The data and specimens submitted by Hudson's Bay Company collectors are therefore less useful as measures of the development of museum anthropology than as indexes of the methodological and theoretical orientations of the new discipline. Northern collectors responded to demands for empirical verification of the nomothetic, as well as to the expropriating tendencies of museums, but increased anthropological accessions were also indicative of the systematization of collecting procedures that Smithsonian scientists had earlier applied to the zoological sciences. Collectors sent examples of native technology to the Smithsonian because those were the specimens needed to test the hypothesis that the aboriginal inhabitants of North America represented an analogous phase of an earlier stage of European civilization, and because Smithsonian scientists specifically requested the collection of certain items.

Gibbs's "Instructions for Archaeological Investigations in the U. States" established standards like those introduced by the field guides written during the 1850s and 1860s by Baird, Brewer, LeConte, Clemens, Loew, and Osten Sacken for zoological collecting, conservation, and documentation. They informed volunteer collectors of anthropologists' needs and interests, directing their activities accordingly. By 1863, formalized directions were also disseminated to facilitate descriptive or ethnographic studies of "primitive man"; Gibbs's second pamphlet reflected his personal interest in cultural attributes and historical linguistics, as well as broader interests in the origins, migration routes, and geographical distribution of North American native peoples. Aboriginal life was to be examined, documented, and, when possible, conserved through collection, in order to reconstruct a "moving panorama of America in the older time."[17] Examinations of trading systems, work habits, physical prowess, and immorality were joined by broader-based examinations of native economics and by studies of social and political organization, law, war, customs, measurement systems, transportation methods, housing, food sources, clothing styles, general physiognomic descriptions, and the medical, industrial, and communicative arts. Tribal names, territorial boundaries, and demographic estimates were also requested. Ethnographic documentation, like collecting, was presented as a form of cultural preservation, and the scientific community assumed that those who could provide information would do so dutifully.

Bernard Rogan Ross accepted his obligation willingly. When asked, he recorded information on the Dene. Ross also agreed with contemporary predictions of the imminent demise of an anachronistic way of life:

> Ethnology is but a modern *science,* and the former habits, customs, and traditions of many tribes are completely lost to the world: while even now the aboriginal races, brought into contact in almost every region with whites, Missionaries and pseudo or real civilization, have imperceptibly lost their ancient ideas, feelings and traditions, and notwithstanding their Asiatic tenacity, insensibly acquired the manners of the dominant race.[18]

Ross's viewpoint conforms to that held by nineteenth-century ethnologists and undoubtedly reflects his connection with Gibbs. Even before Gibbs's instructions for ethnological and philological work were published in 1863, Gibbs had recommended that Ross prepare a descriptive account on northern aboriginal people for the Smithsonian Institution.[19] Ross had obviously made an impression on Gibbs when they first met in 1857 while Gibbs was working as geologist and naturalist with the North West Boundary Survey

Commission, and it is inconceivable that Gibbs would have passed up an opportunity to discuss the importance of ethnography with Ross. The northern trader was too well situated to be overlooked as a future fieldworker.

Although Ross agreed with scientists who argued for the expeditious and comprehensive collection of archaeological specimens, ethnographic data, and ethnological artifacts, he was not motivated by the humanitarianism that permeated nineteenth-century anthropology.[20] Ross undoubtedly understood his contemporary's view of the tragedy that aboriginal Americans faced, but an essay he wrote on the Dene shows that he had little sympathy for the reformer's program; he felt little remorse over the anticipated disappearance of native culture or society.

Ross's essay was published in the Smithsonian *Annual Report* (1866), along with two other northern ethnographies. Strachan Jones described various elements of Kutchin sociocultural organization, and William L. Hardisty wrote a similar essay on the Loucheux.[21] Hardisty, the son of a Hudson's Bay Company fur trader and an Algonkian woman, tended to describe the Loucheux sympathetically, but all three accounts were substantially subjective. Hardisty and Jones were less patronizing and accusatory than Ross, however.

Ross's attempts at objectivity were futile. He lorded his supposed superiority over what were often depicted as subjects barely deserving his consideration. And he never denied himself the pleasure of a deprecatory comment. Scattered throughout Ross's account were statements that often started out innocently enough but concluded with condemnation.[22] For example, in Ross's assessment of the physical attributes and fitness of the Dene people, he made the following statements:

> The prevailing complexion may, with propriety, be said to be of a dirty yellowish ochre tinge, ranging from a smoky brown to a tint as fair as that of many half-caste Europeans.

> The Tinneh are far from a healthy race. The causes of death proceed rather from weakness of constitution and hereditary taint rather than from epidemic diseases, though, when the latter do come, they make great havoc.

Like all hunter tribes these people have the senses of sight and hearing in perfection, while, owing to the dirtiness of their habits, that of smell is greatly blunted.

Ross also had much to say on Dene morality, most of it negative. For example:

Few of the moral faculties are possessed in any remarkable degree by the eastern Tinneh. They are tolerably honest, not bloodthirsty or cruel; but this is, I suppose, the extent, as they are confirmed liars, far from being chaste.

As a whole the race under consideration is unwarlike. . . . On examination of the subject closely, I am disposed to consider that this peaceful disposition proceeds more from timidity than from any actual disinclination to shed blood.

The instinct of love of offspring, common to the lower animals, exists strongly among these people, but considerably modified by the selfishness which is so conspicuous a feature in their character.

Jones was less judgmental than Ross. He slavishly followed the format suggested by Gibbs, never exhibiting any literary aspirations or any inclination for embellishment. Jones put little effort into the construction of his narrative, focusing instead upon relaying all pertinent data. He responded clearly, without hyperbole, to the topics identified by Gibbs. The following extract demonstrates the types of information Gibbs viewed as necessary to describe "primitive" governments:

Government—Is the tribe commanded by the same chief or chiefs in peace and in war, or by different ones? What is the extent of a chief's authority; and how does he acquire it, by birth or by the choice of the people? What are the insignia of his office, and what his privileges? Who are entitled to speak in the councils of the tribe? What laws have they; for instance, what are the punishments for theft, for adultery, for murder; and by whom are punishments inflicted?[23]

Jones's answers to Gibbs's questions were concise and unimaginative:

Government.—They are governed by the same chiefs in peace and in war. The authority of a chief is very limited, for the Indians are very unruly, and not at all disposed to submit to authority. The chiefs are chosen either on account of their wisdom or courage, and not at all on account of birth. They have no insignia of office, and as for privileges they have all that they can take, and none that the others can withold [*sic*] from them. The chiefs and old men are all who are entitled to speak in council, but any young man will not hesitate to get up and give his seniors the benefit of his wisdom.

Law.—They have no law; or, rather, the injured party takes the law into his own hand. For theft, little or no punishment is inflicted; for adultery, the woman only is punished, being beaten and sometimes thrown off by her husband, and instances are not wanting of the woman being put to death; for murder, the friends or relations of the murdered man revenge his death; but if a medicine man is paid to kill him, and the man happens to die, the medicine man is innocent, and the one who paid him is the guilty one.[24]

The ethnography written by Jones was admittedly less entertaining than accounts written by Ross and Hardisty, but the economy and restraint of Jones's style gave his account an air of objectivity that made his essay more compelling as a piece of scientific research. Like Ross, Jones could not resist offering his opinion on the physical attractiveness of his subjects, but his comments were usually less critical than those made by Ross; his contempt for the native population, less pronounced. Jones's essay therefore illustrates the genre that emerged when the first generation of social scientists deliberately attempted to produce a more objective ethnography. Even during the 1860s, objective description was beginning to replace subjective narration as the idiom of scholarly ethnography, and it was this transition that ensured that the authoritativeness or expertise of trained anthropologists would be grounded in a comprehensive or pluralistic approach to the description of unfamiliar, foreign, or exotic cultures.[25]

All three essays reflect the recording procedures being developed by scientists at midcentury, however. The three men followed Gibbs's instructions fairly closely rather than conforming to the literary conventions of the pre-ethnographic accounts written by explorers, travelers, missionaries, and fur traders.[26] Stylistic differences in the essays composed by Ross, Hardisty, and Jones were marginal rather than fundamental. There were, of course, minor differences between their accounts. Ross was the most articulate, but he was also more opinionated and anecdotal than either Jones or Hardisty. Jones wrote the most objective description of native life, whereas Hardisty's essay was the most empathetic. Hardisty did not dwell on native physical characteristics or descriptions of how native people satisfied physiological needs; he instead focused on Loucheux social and political relations, religious beliefs, and language. Hardisty described the Loucheux as a "commercial people," barbarous but sociable and having well established rules of conduct. He provided many English-Loucheux translations, particularly when repeating Loucheux legends. Derisive remarks surfaced occasionally, but his prose was remarkably free from value-laden terminology.

All three essays were biased to a certain extent, but they nevertheless provided invaluable information, previously overlooked or underappreciated, regarding native culture and society. Ross, Hardisty, and Jones were intimately familiar with the observed cultures. Each trader had lived in a northern outpost surrounded by natives for more than a decade before writing his account. Their lives were interwoven with those of northern peoples, and they were privy to information that was inaccessible to visitors. They were intimately familiar with native society and thus capable of responding comprehensively to the Smithsonian circulars.[27] All that Smithsonian scientists had to do was to ask the right questions.

The essays are important for yet another reason. They reflect the methodological assumptions and intellectual orientation that was developing within the emergent social sciences. The Smithsonian did not instruct the Hudson's Bay Company trader-collectors to record information for the immediately utilitarian reasons underlying previous descriptions of North American native peoples. The Smithsonian was not interested in seeking out or making peace with native peoples. It was not observing the native population so as to learn about native survival skills or to obtain the food, shelter, and geographical information needed to expedite exploration in foreign and unfamiliar lands.[28] Nor were the northern ethnographies compiled to facilitate the fur trade or missionization. The Mackenzie River ethnographies were written in response to one of the earliest attempts to objectify anthropology. The procedures outlined by Gibbs represented one of the first deliberate steps taken by anthropologists to emancipate their discipline from a reliance on the secondhand and indiscriminate information thus far obtained from travelers, missionaries, colonial administrators, and fur traders.

Anthropologists such as Gibbs's colleague, the noted Iroquoian specialist Lewis H. Morgan, also benefited from efforts made by northern collectors to satisfy scientific dictates. MacFarlane received Morgan's "Circular in Reference to the Degrees of Relationship among Different Nations,"[29] and in 1863 he informed Baird that he had found linguistic evidence supporting Morgan's distinction between consanguineal and affinal relationships. Mac-Farlane had allegedly discovered that the native people living near Forts Liard and Good Hope possessed the Ganowanian kinship system found among the Iroquoians Morgan had examined; he was prevented from supplying similar data on the Loucheux and "Esquimaux" only because he lacked an interpreter.[30] Morgan did, however, receive information on the Loucheux Indians from W. L. Hardisty. Less sure of his contribution to anthropology than MacFarlane was, Hardisty was nevertheless credited with supplying data for Morgan's studies of kinship and social structure.[31]

Scientific imperatives were not, of course, value-free. But the Hudson's Bay Company ethnographies represent more than the substitution of one form of subjectivity for another. By midcentury, ethnographic studies were increasingly undertaken for epistemological reasons. Simple curiosity about "primitive" people, as well as overt economic and religious concerns, had been subverted by supposedly more important and justifiable reasons. Moreover, assessments of native societies had expanded to include many elements. The contents of the essays written by Ross, Jones, and Hardisty consisted of information recorded in response to anthropological needs, just as the style of their essays reflected changing textual conventions.

Northern documentary and material collections sent to the Smithsonian were important because they were used in some of the first scientific analyses of "primitive" culture, but the role of the Hudson's Bay Company traders and native peoples in obtaining the Smithsonian collections was also noteworthy. Field investigations would soon be performed by trained anthropologists and would become de facto evidence of the measure of an anthropologist's commitment and capabilities.[32] By adhering to Gibbs's instructions, northern traders and trappers participated in early attempts to rationalize anthropological data collecting processes. Northerners formed one of the earliest corps of collectors specifically instructed to collect cultural artifacts for scientific purposes, and their participation in a systematic and directed field program was as important to the development of the social sciences in North America as were their impressive contributions. Their efforts fell midway between those of the professional anthropologist and those of the pre-ethnographers who collected data only sporadically for reasons often quite irrelevant to anthropological studies. They were informed rather than informing, directed rather than directive. Their activities and their motives differed markedly from those of their predecessors, however. The activities of Hudson's Bay Company trader-collectors such as Ross, MacFarlane, Jones, Lockhart, and Hardisty represented a transitional phase in the development of the discipline of anthropology, and their participation in the Smithsonian programs was indispensable to that development. For that reason, Hudson's Bay Company collectors were welcomed into the scientific community that developed around the Smithsonian.

6

❧

RECOGNITION AND REWARD

In 1863 Bernard Rogan Ross went to Washington to visit the Smithsonian and to meet Baird personally. Baird was away when Ross arrived, but Kennicott, who was identifying and cataloguing the northern specimens that he and the Mackenzie River collectors had sent south earlier, immediately put Ross to work assisting him. Setting aside his earlier misgivings about the arrogant trader, Kennicott did his best to make Ross feel welcome and needed: "[Ross] is in very good spirits—extremely conducive and jolly and proposes investigating zoology generally and ornithology particularly—we will endeavor to keep him interested and amused and [I'll] get him to work on the eggs tomorrow."[1] Indeed, Kennicott was surprised to discover that keeping company with Ross was less taxing than he had expected. Civility prevailed despite differences of opinion, as Kennicott noted:

> [Ross's] eggs—they are in a villanious [*sic*] confusion[,] the numbers having sometimes been changed three times and requiring no small work to hunt out the parentage etc—But I reckon we will get it straightened out. I'm merely labelling them and putting on the references to female—Ross is working like a brick and is very conducive—(we'll have to order another ——l of ale tomorrow!)

He insists on making some rather queer identifications of eggs but we can settle it all properly ere they are finally recorded.[2]

Kennicott had not had a change of heart. Nor was his goodwill indicative of his faith in Ross's capabilities as a taxonomist or of his affection for the trader. Kennicott simply treated Ross with the courtesy due someone who had donated as many specimens as Ross had.

So did Joseph Henry. Evincing a certain elitism, Henry believed that fieldworkers like Ross were intellectually and socially limited, unable to perform the more theoretical and synthetic tasks necessary to analyze the raw data that they collected.[3] Nevertheless, Henry welcomed the northern collector and even provided him with a room in his family's quarters at the Smithsonian. Although Ross was far removed from the social and intellectual sphere to which the secretary of the Smithsonian belonged, the Henry family entertained him during his 10-day stay in Washington. Ross was also treated hospitably by Kennicott and the other field naturalists who were staying at the Smithsonian Castle while working on their specimens. During his stay in Washington, Ross usually dined with Kennicott and the other collectors.[4] When Baird returned home on the day before Ross's departure, Ross gladly deviated from his adopted routine to dine with Baird at his home.[5]

Naturalists and collectors in from the field could often be found dining at the assistant secretary's table, exchanging news, and discussing future projects.[6] Opening his home to fieldworkers was an expression of friendship and collegiality and was a part of the nurturing process that converted enthusiastic hobbyists into productive and loyal fieldworkers. It was also a way of expressing appreciation for the contributions made by poorly remunerated or volunteer naturalists and fieldworkers. And Baird was indeed indebted to northerners like Ross.

In Baird's capable hands, such debts could be used to advantage.[7] Recognition and remuneration for past efforts obliged collectors to press on, and Baird never begrudged collectors favors within his power. He gladly acknowledged past efforts and generously offered to do anything he could in anticipation of future endeavors. The Hudson's Bay Company collectors were drawn, often quite willingly, into the web of reciprocity by which the scientific community, and the inadequately endowed Smithsonian in particular, functioned.[8]

Although the collection, preservation, and packing of specimens were generally relegated to the native collectors who would trade their time and skills for money or goods, the documentation, measurement, and identification that were to accompany the specimens were undertaken by the men who expected recognition due persons who had made valuable contributions to science. MacFarlane, Ross, Lockhart, and Jones all took up science as a recreational pursuit, professing a disinterest in receiving credit for their collections, but they believed that their contributions were advancing science, and they quickly eschewed the recreational imperatives that had first motivated them. Science became a serious business. Although these men bore responsibility for prosecuting the fur trade in one of the most lucrative regions of North America, they were status-poor within the Hudson's Bay Company hierarchy; with the exception of Ross, they were all clerks. They had good reason to look to science for recognition and prestige.

Since the coalition of the Hudson's Bay Company and the North West Company in 1821, there had been few opportunities for illustrious fur trade careers or even advancement within the company. Because the coalition substituted monopoly for competition, numerous employees were rendered redundant. The coalition therefore also reduced mobility between the gentleman and servant classes. Decreased mobility was particularly true for Rupert's Landers—the children of Hudson's Bay Company men and native women—but Europeans could also spend upwards of two decades in the service before being made a clerk or even an apprentice clerk.[9] And clerks had the lowest status of the gentleman class. Although clerks were routinely given charge of posts when their superiors were absent, they did not receive promotion for years or even decades. As privileged positions became increasingly inaccessible, employees could expect to spend an average of 15 to 20 years as a clerk before receiving recognition for responsibilities assumed seasonally. By 1860 a clerk could hope to be promoted to a chief trader only after at least a decade and a half of dedicated service; the position of chief factor was even more inaccessible. The situation was uncomfortable and unacceptable for ambitious and intelligent employees, some of whom eagerly embraced the opportunity to exchange data and specimens for prestige, as well as for Baird's friendship and luxury goods.

Although many of the most active Hudson's Bay Company collectors were clerks and spent years coveting positions of real authority—that is, the position of chief trader or the more powerful chief factor—even men who had obtained a measure of career success, such as Bernard R. Ross, could be dissatisfied with their lot in life. Ross was confident of his power and authority, as is evidenced in a letter to Baird: "The death of Sir George Simpson will not interfere in the least with your operations as respects this District—within its bounds my authority is paramount, except special orders of Council be sent me on any subject which I am bound to obey."[10] Ross's assessment of his function within the Hudson's Bay Company hierarchy was inconsistent with his rank, however. Admittedly, he never underestimated himself or his capabilities, and false expectations may have made him more sensitive to slights, snubs, and the effects of diminished opportunities for advancement within the company.

Ross and the other Mackenzie River collectors undoubtedly labored within a corporate hierarchy that had shrunk and become increasingly rigid since the 1821 merger of the Hudson's Bay Company and the North West Company, but in Ross's case the effects of the restricted socioeconomic mobility associated with the post-1821 trade were complicated by his illicit relationship with an Athapaskan woman. Ross's character and capabilities were attacked because of the liaison, and he believed that he was denied promotion because of it.[11] He therefore attempted to overcome what he perceived as unjustified prejudice against his advancement within the company by simply replacing his native "mistress" with a "proper" wife.[12] He misjudged the situation completely, though. In 1860 he married Christina, the daughter of Chief Factor Donald Ross. As Bernard Ross's superior in 1843, the chief factor had described his employee as "one of the greatest blunderers this country (fertile in such cattle) ever produced."[13] The incompetency that Donald Ross considered characteristic of Bernard's administrative skills no doubt improved with time, but

Bernard Ross had developed little social or political finesse even 17 years later. His marriage to Christina did not advance his career. He retired from the company in 1866, never having risen above the rank of chief trader.

Ross was, however, consistently referred to as Chief Factor Ross by Smithsonian scientists. The usage occurred too often to have been accidental. Kennicott had written Baird describing Ross's fondness of flattery and of his propensity for self-aggrandizement, and the assistant secretary seldom missed an opportunity to bolster Ross's sense of self-importance. Nor did Baird hesitate to send Ross and other northerners more tangible rewards for their work in the field. Books, newspapers, tobacco, harmonicas, rifles, and ammunition were just some of the goods sent to northern collectors. Alcohol was the gift of choice, though. Baird responded to numerous requests for whiskey—what was euphemistically referred to as "medicine for exiles," that "elevating substance," and the "element of conduction"— including this provocative request from Ross: "The greatest present you can confer on the Gentlemen is to send in a good stock of spirits for preserving *one half not medicated*—as we must get liquor in sub rosa—with this *stimulant* there is no doubt but that you will obtain lots of things."[14] Many gallons of whiskey were sent north during the six years of the most active collecting, although alcohol was illegal in the Mackenzie River District. Baird was willing to ignore the law on behalf of his collectors and his beloved Institution. He managed to send "good whiskey" north by disguising it as denatured alcohol.

Whiskey was shipped to the north in containers soaked in creosote to deceive company officials into believing that it was for preserving specimens, but such precautions were often unnecessary.[15] The Hudson's Bay Company official at Red River, Governor William Mactavish, turned a blind eye to the liquor traffic and Baird's transgressions. Mactavish felt compelled to sanction the importation of alcohol only after Baird had foolishly asked for official permission to send it inward. Mactavish wrote Baird: "[I]t is contrary to rule to send spirits of any kind into McKenzie River except for medicinal purposes, so that if as a medical man you consider Hardistys ailments require something of the kind I may

tell you that packages for the Companys officers are never subjected to examination by us."[16] Such cooperation was, of course,
appreciated, and Baird's offer to reciprocate was taken up by Mactavish. The governor asked Baird to inquire into the purchase of a
small press, which he planned to use to combat the anti–Hudson's
Bay Company bias found in the settlement's only English-
language newspaper—the *Nor'wester.*[17]

Many items went north as a result of the Smithsonian connection, but books were one of the most common articles received by
northern collectors.[18] Hundreds of volumes were sent to more than
15 individuals, to post libraries, and to the HBC's corporate headquarters in London, England. Recipients of books from Baird
included Donald Gunn, William Mactavish, John Reid, James
Lockhart, Robert Campbell, Charles Gaudet, Roderick Ross Mac-
Farlane, Laurence Clarke, James Dunlop, William Hardisty, Nicol
Taylor, Alexander Mackenzie, and, of course, Bernard Rogan
Ross.[19] Novels and poetry by authors such as Dickens, Spenser,
Burns, and Byron, as well as scholarly and popular studies in
history, philosophy, and theology, were bestowed upon the northerners. Smithsonian publications and other scientific literature,
including Baird's ornithological monographs and government
publications such as the multivolume *Pacific Railroad Survey
Reports,* figured prominently in the shipments of books.

Baird's choice of reading material also meant that rewards for
past efforts could facilitate future fieldwork. The instructional
pamphlets, manuals, directions, articles, and monographs both
acknowledged and enabled fieldwork. Northerners were gratified
to receive Baird's catalogues of birds and mammals or Kennicott's
articles on Illinois mammals, for example, but besides being
enlightening and a pleasure to own, they also served as guides in
the identification and description of specimens.

Baird similarly supplied his collectors with the apparatus and
materials necessary for fieldwork.[20] Although the Hudson's Bay
Company collectors were often forced to make do with homegrown
substitutes for the three dozen or so items listed in the Smithsonian circular, Baird did his best to supply them with the recommended equipment and supplies: pencils, parchment, fishing line
and hooks, small seines, pocket scoop net and casting net, alcohol,

arsenic, alum, saltpeter, tartar emetic, strychnine, camphor, cotton stuffing, cotton twine, butcher knife, scissors, needles, thread, common pins, blank labels, portfolio for carrying plants, plant-drying press, botanical blotting paper, small bottles, geological hammer, double-barreled gun, rifle, fine shot, pocket case of dissecting instruments, mineralogical blowpipe, pocket vial for insects, ether, insect pins, cork-lined boxes, a pocket notebook with metallic paper, two wooden chests or two leather panniers, two copper kettles, six tin preserving cans, an iron wrench, two inflatable India-rubber bags, and small lino, cotton, or mosquito-netting bags.[21] These items were indispensable to proper field studies. Thus it was in Baird's interest to outfit northern collectors as fully as possible, but Baird's care and attention in doing so were unprecedented. Other organizations and individuals had sought northern specimens, but few had devoted the time and the attention needed to ensure that lay collectors properly prepared natural history specimens.

When Roderick MacFarlane requested materials for the preservation and packing of specimens, Baird responded promptly.[22] Baird did not doubt MacFarlane's capability to assess and order supplies. Indeed, MacFarlane's efforts on behalf of the Smithsonian impressed even Joseph Henry, whose antipathy to the Natural History Department was legendary, if not entirely accurate, and Baird would not have refused MacFarlane any request.[23] The prodigious collector usually asked for Baird's assistance only hesitantly, however. During the 1860s, he asked for little more than those articles specifically required for the preparation of specimens. He stated repeatedly his dread of inconveniencing or troubling the assistant secretary and once offered to withdraw an application for the redistribution of some of his collections if such a request was "against either the custom or rules of the Institution to present objects of Natural History to individuals."[24] Once convinced that such requests did not conflict with Smithsonian policies, MacFarlane asked again that Baird redirect his specimens. In 1865 he asked Baird to forward specimens to Oxford University and the Natural History Society of Montreal, and in 1866 he requested that some of his collection go to the Edinburgh Museum of Science and Art.[25]

MacFarlane abstained from seeking any recognition for his efforts until 1907, when advanced age and an inadequate income prompted him to ask for financial compensation in the form of a Smithsonian or U.S. government pension. Negotiating on his behalf was Winnipeg lawyer Hugh John Macdonald, the son of Canada's first prime minister, Sir John A. Macdonald. MacFarlane was, however, unsuccessful in his bid to obtain a pension from either source. The Institution rejected his request, falling back on policies established by Joseph Henry in the 1850s: Neither specimens nor data were to be purchased outright, nor was the Institution allowed to make contractual agreements with collectors. C. D. Walcott, secretary of the Smithsonian in 1918, stated in one of the final exchanges between the Smithsonian and MacFarlane's attorney: "[T]he only recognition that can be made of his cooperation and interest is in the form of references thereto in the publications of the Institution, and this has already been done many times."[26]

Walcott was right. MacFarlane's assistance was acknowledged more frequently in Baird's ornithological monographs than that of any other North American contributor. Entries in *A History of North American Birds* and *The Water Birds of North America*, for example, note the contributions made by the Hudson's Bay Company collectors and by MacFarlane in particular. Field collectors' efforts were credited exhaustively by the authors of those volumes—Baird, Brewer, and Ridgway. Descriptions of the geographical distribution and habitat, the measurement and coloration, and the breeding and nesting habits of each species include memoranda regarding the field notes and physical specimens used. MacFarlane and Ross were individually mentioned not less than 200 times in the five volumes making up the two studies, and the contributions of other northern collectors, including Donald Gunn, George Barnston, Strachan Jones, James Lockhart, John Reid, John Mackenzie, James Sibbeston, Laurence Clarke, James Flett, and Charles Gaudet, were also noted many times. Their special contributions were given added recognition in 1891, when an entire volume of the *Proceedings of the United States National Museum* (Volume 14) was devoted to their ornithological collections. Roderick Ross MacFarlane wrote a brief introduction to

"Notes on and List of Birds and Eggs Collected in Arctic America, 1861–1866," which was an abridged account of the earlier monographs identifying the northern memoranda and specimens that Baird, Brewer, and Ridgway used in their studies of North American birds.

Kennicott also appreciated MacFarlane's efforts, and he too did favors for MacFarlane and the other northern collectors once he was back in the United States. After returning to Illinois, Kennicott sent Julian Onion a set of billiard balls, MacFarlane some alcohol, and Lockhart a ring.[27] Kennicott also corresponded with northerners, encouraging them to continue collecting for the Smithsonian by appealing to their sense of duty and their vanity. His flattery became quite lavish at times, placing more importance on scientific achievements than on the contributions made by politicians and corporate managers: "Upon my honor McFarlane I would rather have had the honor of contributing what you and Lockhart have to the history of Arctic zoology than to be a Chief Factor in the H.B.Co or a member of Parliament—The latter would be jolly during life but in the former case my name would be immortal among naturalists."[28]

MacFarlane was initially reluctant to accept such accolades, but he did eventually accept Kennicott's assessment of his work:

> Should your own and Professor Baird's future letters to me prove as flattering as those I have been accustomed to receive of late, I really must believe, what I have not hitherto done, that I am doing something in the way of advancing the interests of Science— however, as I myself experience much pleasure in collecting objects of Natural History, I shall continue the occupation, equally regardless of praise as of censure. As for writing anything for *publication*—I'll know more of the subject than I do now, ere Ive persuaded to attempt anything of the kind; as to the brief notes accompanying the specimens I care not what use may be made of them, as they are, I think, correct in the *little* they say. But enough of this for the present.[29]

In accepting their praise, MacFarlane always seemed to retain a certain charming humility, although he did agree to write up his natural history notes for publication. He wrote some articles on northern natural history, and his work on northern zoology was appended to a monograph entitled *Through the Mackenzie Basin*.[30] MacFarlane wrote a pamphlet on North American mammals for the U.S. National Museum, and the text on northern ornithology in the 1891 *Proceedings of the United States National Museum* was originally published by the Historical and Scientific Society of Manitoba.[31]

Bernard Rogan Ross was also a published author, but he needed no convincing of the importance of his work, as he demonstrated in an 1860 letter to Baird: "Accompanying this are a few notes on the Mammals sent, it was my intention to have sent a few remarks on every species forward: but the multiplicity of my avocations prevented me—I hope however in time to pass the whole fauna of the District in review in the style of my treatise on the fur animals with colored photographs of every species described."[32] A year later he made a similar comment: "It is my intention to send you out a complete collection of the arts manufactures dresses etc. of the Indians wh copious notes—These are partly written in a popular form, and which you can make available for some scientific periodical sending me a few copies if they be worth publishing."[33] In addition to an article on the Dene in the 1866 Smithsonian *Annual Report*, Ross had a zoological article published in 1862 in *Natural History Review* (London) and six articles published in *Canadian Naturalist and Geologist*.[34]

Jones, Hardisty, Lockhart, and Gunn also had articles published. Ethnographic accounts written by Hardisty, Jones, and Gunn were printed in the *Annual Report* of the Smithsonian, as was an account of one of Gunn's egging expeditions.[35] Lockhart's "Notes on the Habits of the Moose in the Far North of British America in 1865" was published in *Proceedings of the United States National Museum* (1890).

George Barnston was the only trader-collector recruited by Kennicott who did not publish with the Smithsonian. He was, he confessed, too much the patriot to want to establish himself within the Republican scientific community.[36] He was a member of the Natural History Society of Montreal and a presenting member at the inaugural meeting of the Botanical Society of Montreal.[37] A reputable author on scientific subjects, he had one article in the

British ornithological journal *Ibis* and nine articles in *Canadian Naturalist and Geologist*. Four of the articles published in the Canadian journal appeared before 1860; the other five were published between 1860 and 1875.[38] Not one word written by Barnston was ever printed by the Smithsonian.

Barnston's sympathies rested with the British and Canadian scientific communities. His work for the Smithsonian reinforced earlier scientific endeavors; his reputation was established independent of his connection with Baird and Kennicott. Ross and MacFarlane, however, channeled their activities through the American institution. Although Ross established a working relationship with both British and Canadian scientists, MacFarlane's scientific career was due almost entirely to his relationship with the Smithsonian. Both men nevertheless recognized the importance of membership in the societies favored by Barnston.

Ross was especially aware of the prestige associated with formal membership in such organizations. Between 1861 and 1867 he joined five scientific and philosophical societies: the Natural History Society of Montreal, the New York Historical Society, the London Royal Geographical Society, the Anthropological Society of London, and the Hall of the Academy of Natural Sciences of Philadelphia.[39] Becoming a member of the Philadelphia academy was an honor that he actively sought, and he did not hesitate to request Baird's assistance in securing it: "I am preparing an article on the *Anatrace* [Anatidae?] found in this District for the Academy of Sciences, as I do not wish to be a silent member—I enclose it to you, and would feel *very much obliged* if you would look over it first and then forward it with the accompanying letter to Philadelphia."[40] MacFarlane too eventually joined several philosophical and scientific societies: the Royal Geographical Society, the Royal Colonial Institute, the Imperial Institute, the American Ornithological Society, and the National Geographic Society (United States).[41] Both Ross and MacFarlane sought and achieved acceptance from a larger constituency; both were recognized by a community that extended the privilege of membership only in recognition of an ability to advance knowledge.[42] They undoubtedly represented the membership at the lowest level of the scientific community's hierarchy, but they nevertheless obtained access to a largely inaccessible group.[43] Such membership at least partially realized a dream articulated by Ross to Baird as early as 1861: "I wish to make myself a name in the scientific world if possible, and I am sure that you will do all in your power to gain it for me."[44]

Although collecting provided Ross and MacFarlane an opportunity to acquire prestige and status outside the confines of the fur trade, not all northern collectors aspired to formal membership in the scientific community. James Lockhart and Strachan Jones saw their Smithsonian connection in more practical terms. Baird actually offered them an alternative to working for the Hudson's Bay Company—an alternative they both considered. Lockhart and Jones received a furlough in 1867, and while on leave in eastern Canada they traveled to Washington to meet Baird and see the Smithsonian. En route to Washington, they stopped in New York to meet with the secretary of the Western Union Telegraph Company.[45] Western Union had tentatively offered Lockhart a position working on its lines in the Northwest—an offer also extended to Jones—and so both men were more than happy to supply the company with whatever information they could about the Hudson's Bay Company territories. Western Union had been gathering geographical and climatological information on the far north since the summer of 1864, when final plans were being made for the overland telegraph, but by the time Lockhart and Jones arrived at company headquarters, Western Union was reassessing the project. The completion of Cyrus Field's transatlantic cable in the autumn of 1866 made a telegraphic connection to Europe via Bering Strait and Siberia unnecessary. Western Union officially abandoned the overland route on 9 March 1867, and Baird wisely advised Lockhart and Jones to keep their positions with the Hudson's Bay Company.[46]

If Lockhart and Jones were disappointed with Baird's inability to deliver the positions with Western Union, they could not be dissatisfied with his efforts on their behalf. How many could claim that an important American scientist had acted as their agent in securing employment or that the assistant secretary of the Smithsonian Institution had purchased goods on their behalf? By simply responding to requests for goods from the "civilized" world, Baird bestowed upon the isolated northern fur traders a privilege extended to few people.

The assistant secretary extended himself even further on behalf of his field volunteers by corresponding with each and every collector personally. In 1860, for example, he wrote 3,050 letters.[47] Perhaps most important, through his position as the preeminent American ornithologist, he was able to recognize the contributions made by his most productive collectors by naming new species in their honor. Ross's goose (*Chen rossi* [*Chen rossii*]) was named for Ross,[48] and MacFarlane was twice honored—once in scientific nomenclature and once in common terminology. *Falco gyrfalco* var. *sacer* was referred to as MacFarlane's gyrfalcon, and a screech owl has since been named in his honor as *Otus asio macfarlanei*.[49] Baird's colleague Fielding B. Meek also recognized MacFarlane's contributions by naming two fossils after the northern trader (*Zaphrentis mcfarlanei* and *Orthis mcfarlanei*).[50]

The immediacy of tangible remuneration was an undeniably important incentive for many collectors, but social factors also motivated men such as Ross and MacFarlane to collect natural history specimens. Whereas native individuals adopted collecting as a means to increase their purchasing power for American and European goods, status-hungry traders looked to science as a route for bettering their social position. Baird and Kennicott treated collectors such as MacFarlane and Ross as equals. Allowed access to a whole new community, such collectors reveled in their newfound roles. Formal recognition through publication, acknowledgments in scientific monographs, and membership in learned societies, as well as Baird's friendship, encouragement, and praise, repaid their efforts in ways that trading specimens for specie could not. Science had its own reward system, and northern collectors received both institutionalized and interpersonal recognition within the scientific community.[51] That respect and recognition could be substituted for the corporate success that was denied men such as Ross, MacFarlane, Lockhart, and Jones. These men assisted the Smithsonian because scientific activities had social functions that were, in many ways, as important as their epistemological functions.

PART THREE

The Natural Sciences in
Russian America, 1865–1866

7

THE WESTERN UNION TELEGRAPH EXPEDITION

Kennicott and Baird were organizing a second collecting expedition less than two years after Kennicott's return from the Mackenzie River District. Kennicott had always intended on going to Russian America, even after it became clear that he could not travel overland to the northwest coast from the Hudson's Bay Company's posts. In 1864 a means of getting there presented itself. The Western Union Telegraph Company proposed to extend its services to Europe via the northwest coast of America, passing under Bering Strait and through Siberia and Russia. When the company offered Baird an opportunity to send a scientific collector along with its telegraphic expedition, he decided to try to obtain specimens and data once again from Russian America.

Kennicott's 1865 expedition to Russian American was neither a personal triumph nor a scientific success like his earlier trip to the Mackenzie River District. Although he took six friends and associates, recruited specifically because of their interest in science, he was unable to transform their potential into tangible results. The Russian American expedition ostensibly differed little from the earlier trip. Both expeditions focused on the north; both had a mandate to collect natural history specimens; both were dependent on the sponsorship and goodwill of a corporation; and both were manifestations of Smithsonian science. Using the services of a corporate organization to facilitate field studies had proven successful in the Hudson's Bay Company–Smithsonian venture, and Western Union's proposal seemed to present similar possibilities for the advancement of Smithsonian research. But between March 1865, when Kennicott left New York for San Francisco, and May 1866, when he died at Nulato, the young naturalist discovered just how different the two expeditions could be.

Kennicott left New York Harbor on 21 March 1865.[1] Baird and Rev. Sylvester Sewall Cutting, one of Mrs. Baird's cousins and a close personal friend of several of the directors of Western Union, had suggested Kennicott as leader of the scientific corps. Western Union agreed because of Kennicott's reputation as a northern expert. His firsthand knowledge of the north was virtually unequaled outside Rupert's Land and was much needed by Western Union, as Cutting pointed out to Baird:

> I do not believe there will ever be, or can ever be, an earthly revelation of the benefits which you and Kennicott have conferred on the Telegraph enterprise of our Russian Extension friends. Capt. Bulkley has some appreciation of it, so has Judge Palmer, but nobody can know so well as Kennicott and you and I. Things have gone well in the preparations for the exploration since we met Bulkley in New York, and never till then were they otherwise than in hopeless confusion or darkness.[2]

The telegraph company worked hard to persuade Kennicott to go to Russian America, even capitalizing on his relationship with Baird and the Smithsonian. In exchange for Kennicott's knowledge of and presence in Russian America, the company offered Baird a chance to send a corps of field naturalists with its overland expedition.[3]

Western Union was especially interested in obtaining information on the geography and climate of the north, but it also sought Kennicott's opinion on the best route for its new line. Kennicott believed that the Hudson's Bay Company would be willing to subsidize construction of the line for the privilege of using or partly owning it,[4] and both he and Baird suggested building the telegraph through the HBC territory, running it from Fort Garry to Edmonton, through Fort Simpson, and then into Russian America.[5] At first the company agreed with Kennicott and Baird, but by the time that preparations for the expedition were under way, the route had been changed. Western Union chose a route that not only ignored but also contradicted Kennicott's recommendations. The company decided to retain full ownership of the telegraph by building north of the last station on the California State telegraph, a line it had acquired in 1864. The chosen route went north of Portland, through New Westminster and the Fraser River valley, across the Skeena, Nass, and Stikeen rivers, and into Russian America via the Yukon River.[6]

Despite Western Union's disregard for his opinion, and despite numerous other factors that were quite unrelated to the expedition but nevertheless detracted from its appeal, Kennicott agreed to head up the scientific corps. He did not really want to go, because he was already too busy. He was raising money, finding facilities, and developing collections for his own museum at the Chicago Academy of Sciences.[7] In addition, because all he knew about the north had been learned at the expense of the Hudson's Bay Company, he felt a certain obligation to obtain the company's permission before going anywhere in the north on behalf of another corporation.[8] Kennicott was persuaded to put aside his own work for that of the Smithsonian only after a fire at the Castle in January 1865. Until that point, he had wavered between going with Western Union and staying in Chicago. After the fire, he offered his services to Baird unreservedly. He would work in Washington or in the north—wherever he could do the most good for Smithsonian science. He wrote Baird: "[I]f your future plans will best be furthered by my making big arctic collections why I'll perform impossibilities in the way of collecting."[9]

Unfortunately, although Kennicott's commitment to Baird and the Smithsonian was unshakable, Western Union's commitment to science was neither clear nor sincere. The company intended to use Kennicott's scientific knowledge for its own purposes, offering only to substantiate that he was, in fact, "doing" scientific work so that he could raise funds for "his" expedition from members of the Chicago Academy and other philanthropists.[10]

Once committed, Kennicott handpicked a small group of men to help him collect natural history specimens and to carry out the surveying work expected by Western Union. As chief of the Russian American Division, Kennicott was responsible for finding the actual route through Russian America. Western Union therefore agreed to hire J. T. Rothrock, Ferdinand Bischoff, Henry Bannister, Henry Elliott, and Charles Pease, who were offered $30 per month, as were the other members of the telegraphic expedition. William Healey Dall initially joined the scientific corps as Kennicott's assistant, and G. M. Maynard went as a volunteer, paying his own passage. Rothrock and Maynard were recent acquaintances, whereas Bannister and Elliott were longtime family friends, but Kennicott considered Maynard as one of the "four good men and true," along with Bannister, Bischoff, and Dall. Bannister was the son of a Methodist clergyman from Evanston, and Elliott was a young man from Cleveland whom Kennicott referred to as the "Irrepressible." Described by Kennicott as a "glorious old fellow," Bischoff had been hired to work in the museum at the Chicago Academy of Sciences. Dall had been recommended for the expedition by Colonel Foster, his supervisor at the Iron Cliffs Company, where he worked as a clerk, explorer, and geological assistant.[11]

It took the party 35 days to reach San Francisco traveling via ship and crossing the Isthmus of Panama on wagons and mules. After arriving on the west coast, the members of the expedition discovered that they would have to stay in San Francisco longer than the projected few days. Kennicott complained bitterly about the delay, but the two-and-a-half-month stopover was less of a hardship than he described. The men had much to do before their expedition could depart safely for the north. Although both Kennicott and Dall lamented the inactivity and lethargy they experienced in San Francisco, as well as the "dissipation" of the men engaged by Western Union, their days were full.[12] Because Colonel Bulkley, the engineer in chief of the entire expedition, wanted to conduct affairs according to military rules and regulations, everything had to be done, as Kennicott stated, to satisfy the "red tapists" who ran the "Circumlocution Office." Nevertheless, certain things did have to be done. Outfits had to be checked, added to, and packed up. Directions for scientific work were copied for distribution among the men. Uniforms and insignia were designed, ordered, and fitted. And men had to be hired, then detailed to one of the three divisions (British Columbia, Russian America, and Siberia) responsible for building the overland telegraph.

Additionally, the time in San Francisco was not entirely unpleasant. Although Kennicott and Dall viewed the city as a den of iniquity—filled with gamblers, prostitutes, and drunkards—it was not without its charms even for upstanding young men. They passed their days collecting and processing natural history specimens, going to the theater and to music recitals, playing chess, working at the California Academy of Sciences, and visiting the homes of academy members. Kennicott even developed a romantic interest in a young woman named Olga. She was the daughter of Captain Klinkofstrom, the Russian consul in San Francisco. In July, Kennicott considered asking Olga to be his wife.[13] He was, however, still unmarried when the expedition left the city.

Kennicott was anxious to go north in time for the bird breeding season, and with the delay, his anxiety turned into anger and then depression.[14] In addition to missing the most important season for collecting, Kennicott found that his plans for natural history seemed entirely in doubt on several occasions. While in San Francisco, he had a dispute with Bulkley, and his relations with the other officers were less than cordial. Kennicott and Dall both believed that William B. Hyde, a lieutenant colonel in the California governor's office, along with Dr. Henry Fisher, the expedition surgeon, and a Mr. O'Donohue, had been trying to obtain the position of assistant engineer for Hyde, thereby making him second in command of the entire expedition.[15] Their plans were jeopardized when Kennicott arrived in San Francisco, however. The company had worked hard to get Kennicott to join the expedition, and it was logical that he would be given a position of authority. Although Kennicott denied any interest in such a position and was made only a "major," he felt confident that he could have done it.[16] In July, Kennicott wrote a lengthy and impassioned, if not entirely illuminating, account of the dispute:

> [R]ecently I have learned that Hyde has systematically injured me with the Col on every occasion and has repeatedly interfered with my plans. . . . He has been a perfect firebrand in the whole expe-

dition community here. And together with a chap named O'Donohue from Rochester (whom I offended by a well merited rebuke
when I first arrived here) managed for a while get me a bad name
with all the officers as well as Bulkley. I now think some of my own
party were less to blame than I thought. That is they were certainly
told many lies about me. . . . [T]he other officers are [now] beginning to discover that instead of being the tyrannical, quarrelsome,
incompetent and untruthful chap I was represented to be I am in
fact not such an utterly disagreeable fellow after all.[17]

Kennicott's stay in San Francisco was not boring, but it was
wearing.

The falling-out between Kennicott and Bulkley had serious
repercussions for Kennicott's scientific work. Although there was a
vague understanding that the members of the scientific corps
would serve on any or all of the three divisions of the expedition,
most of Kennicott's men abandoned him prematurely for the British Columbia division, fearing that their allegiance to Kennicott
would jeopardize their positions on the telegraphic expedition.
Such a prospect was troubling because they had all been made
second lieutenants with a starting salary of $30 per month and had
been promised an increase to $50 per month once the real work
began in July.[18] Their defection left Kennicott disillusioned and
disheartened. Charles Pease was the only member of Kennicott's
original corps to remain with him from start to finish. The
"major" therefore had to find new assistants who would be loyal
and dependable. Kennicott persuaded Bulkley to allow him to
choose 10 more "good men," and he invested both time and
money to ensure their loyalty, as Dall wrote to Baird: "[Kennicott]
spent at least two thirds his years salary during the last few weeks of
our stay in Frisco, in lending these men money, treating them like
brothers and endeavoring to create a clannish feeling among them
that would carry them through difficulty and danger which they
will meet."[19]

Kennicott called the men the Carcajous, meaning "wolver-
ines." William Ennis was hired after telling Dall, "[A]dventure
and my love of roaming alone induced me to take the trip."[20]
Ennis, himself unemployed before his encounter with Dall, was
immediately given responsibility for hiring 50 local men for the

expedition. When given a choice between the Yukon or the British Columbia expedition, Ennis chose to go on the former because of the "novelties" of the trip. He was placed in charge of the scientific expedition's journal, undoubtedly because he had at one time been a secretary to one of the commodores in the United States Navy. Joseph Dyer, a former streetcar conductor, was also asked to go to Russian America with Kennicott. His connection to natural history, though slight, probably worked in his favor: He was a cousin of ornithologist John Cassin's. Another streetcar conductor, Thomas Denison, was invited to join the scientific expedition, as were two clerks—George Adams and Fred Smith. Two Canadians were also picked—Frank Ketchum of St. John, New Brunswick, and Mike Lebarge of Quebec. Lebarge acted as interpreter, along with Andrew Gronberg, a Swedish sailor from Sitka, and O. de Bendeleben. Several laborers accompanied Kennicott's party, as well as a quartermaster named James Bean, who was to oversee their outfit at St. Michael's Redoubt. Eventually Henry Bannister, one of the members of the original corps who abandoned Kennicott for the British Columbia expedition, ended up in Russian America. After rejoining Kennicott, he was made meteorological observer at St. Michael's.

Kennicott and his men were given specific orders. Their first priority was to explore the territory between St. Michael's and Grantley Harbor on Norton Sound, over to Fort Yukon—an area of more than 50,000 square miles. They were to determine if the Russian-named Kwichpak River and the English-named Yukon River were one and the same and if building the telegraph along the river would be feasible. Kennicott's orders also contained a contingency plan. If the British Columbian division did not manage to lay cable straight through to the Yukon, he and his men were supposed to travel down into the interior of British Columbia, south of the Yukon River and north of the Stikeen and Dease Lake water system, and reconnoiter with it.[21]

Bulkley did not mention natural history, the Smithsonian Institution, or the Chicago Academy of Sciences in his instructions to Kennicott. Although that gap in his instructions may have been an oversight, implying that specimens could be gathered when time and circumstances permitted, it more likely reflected Western

Union's attitude toward nontelegraphic fieldwork. The company was primarily and rightfully concerned with getting the telegraph up; it needed Kennicott's expertise in both the planning and the execution of the project, but it neither needed nor wanted zoological specimens or data. There was less commitment to scientific research, as defined by Baird and Kennicott, than those two men appreciated in 1864 and 1865. Soon after Kennicott reached St. Michael's, it became apparent that there would be little time, and even less desire on the part of the company, to collect flora and fauna.

Given Western Union's stance on collecting, Kennicott's surprise at discovering he would have little time to collect indicates that there was some confusion over his role in the north. Regardless of whether the misunderstanding was due to Kennicott's obstinacy or to some deceptiveness on the part of the telegraph company, Kennicott was aware by July that little in the way of collecting would be done for some time:

> I have begun to despair of effecting much of anything this fall but shall do my best in Norton Sound, and hope a good deal from old Bischoff and Dall.
>
> I consider that I can do most in the long run for Nat. History by pitching bravely into this winter expedition—Even should I *go up* think Dall, Bulkley and Scammon with the others will carry on the work and the concern ought to reward my efforts even if fatal by carrying out their promises. This winter expedition is certainly purely telegraphic and I think I deserve some credit from the directors for undertaking it—not that I expect much for I never yet knew a corporation with any gratitude.[22]

The hardships Kennicott and his men confronted dashed any remaining hopes of collecting. The weather was harsh, provisions were inadequate, and the men were already overworked just trying to transport provisions and supplies inland to winter quarters, which they sometimes had to build before inhabiting. It was a daily struggle to survive the elements and to meet Colonel Bulkley's expectations. The only significant collecting between the autumn of 1865 and the spring of 1866 was by individuals more favorably situated. Impressive contributions to the Smithsonian Institution were made by William Dall and by Ferdinand Bischoff.

Kennicott had intended to leave Bischoff at St. Michael's to collect while he and the other men went inland to work on the telegraph, but Bischoff became ill en route to St. Michael's and was left at the village of Sitka to recuperate. Although ill, Bischoff was comfortably housed and cared for, and he managed to collect natural history specimens while convalescing.[23] Dall was similarly able to devote some time to collecting. He reported that he collected one day out of 30 while traveling aboard ship in Norton Sound and along the northwest coast. He also collected natural history specimens in southern California.[24] Most of his specimens were marine invertebrates (his specialty), but he did collect some minerals, rocks, and fossils and a few vertebrates. Dall did not do any scientific work on mainland Alaska until spring 1868.

Kennicott's party arrived at St. Michael's on 9 September.[25] By 26 September they were ready to begin their journey to Fort Yukon, but the steamer that Bulkley had given them to move their outfit inland was immobilized by a faulty pipe. Nevertheless, Kennicott and his men left St. Michael's the following day—aboard a 40-foot sailboat borrowed from the Russians. Within days, the river was beginning to freeze over. Kennicott's crew and native boatmen poled, paddled, and pulled the craft upriver amid the setting ice. It was impetuous of Kennicott to attempt to go inland during freeze-up, but he was impatient to get to Fort Yukon. He also knew he had to establish camp at Nulato and Unalakleet, and so expected to be fully occupied until the snow arrived. Kennicott thought his party could travel to Fort Yukon by dogsled and snowshoes by mid-November, but his plans did not materialize as he envisioned them. Kennicott's experience as a northern explorer had landed him the job of chief of the scientific corps and head of the Russian-American Division of the telegraphic expedition, but what he had learned about the north while living at the Hudson's Bay Company posts was of little use when Western Union officials and Bulkley refused to follow his recommendations. Nor was it of much use when he was left to his own devices to cope with the Alaskan environment. He had overcome political intrigues, dissension among his men, and the anxiety caused by the numerous delays between March and July, but he could not overcome the obstacles that confounded his plans after his arrival at St. Michael's.

He faced one problem after another. In addition to the defective steamer, Kennicott found that the provisions that the steamer was supposed to transport were inadequate and inappropriate, as Dall noted: "Part of the outfit which he required was obtained and part not, much was relied on goods sent from New York, in the two vessels dispatched last winter. Part was to be got in Victoria. Part was laughed at and utterly denied through gross ignorance in high quarters."[26] Even before he left San Francisco Kennicott knew his scientific outfit was entirely inadequate—his supply of alcohol and arsenic was limited, and he was not allowed to take even one of Western Union's barometers or sextants with him to Nulato. Kennicott had added to the provisions needed for collecting data and specimens from his own funds,[27] as well as supplementing them from provisions allocated to Captain Scammon, chief of Western Union's marine corps. Kennicott also obtained permission to purchase up to $5,000 worth of goods from the Russian store at St. Michael's. To his dismay, however, he discovered that the telegraph outfit was also short, and he was forced to use his scientific outfit for telegraphic work.

The supply problem originated, in large part, in Bulkley's policy of issuing supplies and rations according to army regulations. Kennicott had objected to that policy, arguing that even when full army rations were purchased (which they had not been), they were insufficient to sustain men working in cold climates.[28] The caloric intake needed for manual labor in the north exceeded that available from the slapjacks (a mixture of flour and water fried in fat), beans, and tea that his men invariably ate. Each man could consume five pounds of meat and half a pound of fat per day, when such supplies were available.[29] Moreover, the uneven distribution of northern game during the winter months meant that fresh meat was an unreliable supplement to their army rations, and Kennicott's party was camped in an area where game was particularly scarce. It was virtually impossible—even for native hunters—to acquire fresh meat there.[30]

The dietary grievances were aggravated by Western Union's shortsightedness in other areas. For example, the clothing supplied by Western Union was unsuited to northern winters. Woolen uniforms provided slight protection from the northern wind, freezing temperatures, and icy dunkings in northern rivers that the men frequently took. Military garb had the advantage of impressing the Russians, but once beyond St. Michael's, that was not an asset. More important, Kennicott warned, military rules would not impress the Kutchin.[31] Other grievances also stemmed from Bulkley's policies. He underfilled requisitions for firearms and ammunition, and he did not supply any fuel, on the assumption that the expedition could collect driftwood for burning.

Poorly outfitted, Kennicott's party spent much of the winter of 1865–66 either starving or freezing. When they could, they stayed with native peoples in their underground winter homes, but the Koyukon people living between Nulato and Unalakleet were also short of food. In 1865–66, large game was unusually scarce, so, except for being more warmly dressed, the Koyukon were not much better off than Kennicott's men. In November, George Adams noticed that some native villages were already out of food: "[T]he Indians seem to be living on nothing[,] which is very cheap living and does not take much trouble to digest."[32] Supplies did not improve before spring. For the most part, Kennicott and his men spent the winter trying to stay alive. They freighted what few provisions they had from place to place and searched for natives who could sell them provisions or provide information about the country. Some exploratory and surveying work was completed for Western Union, but not one specimen was collected from the mainland for the Smithsonian Institution or the Chicago Academy of Sciences.

By March, Kennicott was planning another expedition to Fort Yukon. His men had been unable to travel inland to any great extent because the winter snow had proved much softer than stated by the Russians. Neither snowshoes nor dogs were really useful unless the snow was hard. During the first few months of 1866, snow conditions lost their relevancy, however. Both dogs and dog feed were unavailable. By the end of April it was obvious that the group's departure would be postponed until well after spring breakup. Even in May, Adams wrote, the snow was like quicksand. Kennicott's men could travel only 5 to 10 miles per day, instead of the usual 50 or more. As Adams put it, they were at the "height of misery."[33]

Kennicott must have been disappointed that he had not collected anything except while traveling across the Isthmus of Panama the previous year and that he would miss the best part of another collecting season on the Yukon.[34] Theoretically, he could have collected natural history specimens around Nulato, but because he had promised to do exploratory work for the telegraph between St. Michael's and Fort Yukon, he was otherwise occupied. Especially after the attacks Hyde and Fisher had leveled against his leadership and competency, he refused to renege on his commitment to Western Union. He went north feeling the need to prove himself, and he was loath to admit defeat. Thinking his honor was at stake, he wrote, for example: "I'm going to *succeed fully by God if it is only to put myself in a position to punish* those who have been the cause of this absurd outfit which is furnished me," and "I don't like reporting failures. I will yet effect some good work for science or finish my days in the north."[35]

Kennicott's attitude was childish, but it was also much more. It was in keeping with previous behavior.[36] Kennicott had always been somewhat sickly, and after returning home from the Mackenzie River District in 1862, he spent several months recuperating—or, as he put it, "vegetating"—at his parents' home in Illinois. His indispositions were mainly emotional. In the autumn of 1863, he experienced a period of especially severe depression, which he described to Baird:

> I'm about as dead as usual come to life a little on frosty nights, but have done no work whatever. Dr Reilly my brother-in-law is at home on sick leave and has been badgering me to make me commence writing a popular account of Life in the north—But it dont seem to get written. I'm as contented as a fig here and not quite as useful. I dont know whether [I'll] work any when cold weather comes or not. I fully realize the disgrace and sin of my idleness but thats about all the good it does—My mother tries to make me write and wont let me work with my brothers (on those rare occasions when I want to) and wont let me look at a novel. So I play with the

baby, admire Cora and Alice, or lie on the lounge and watch the leaves fall from the trees.

My present feelings on the subject of Natural History are that it is a humbug—that is when I think of it at all I have a faint impression to that effect—I never have strong impressions of any kind, and very much dislike thinking on any subject.

I have also a faint impression that at this rate I shall go to the D——l, that is so far as any usefulness is concerned.

In the same faint kind of a way I fancy that if I were at the Smithsonian and you told me to do anything I should do it.

Now I certainly don't feel the slightest inclination to do anything that requires any mental exertion; But, making a great effort, and bringing what little reason I have to bear upon the subject, I'm forced to acknowledge that though much less pleasant it would be far better for me to be at work on *something* at the Smithsonian than stagnating here.

But I have a dim kind of a recollection that I not only have no money but am a good deal in debt—and that too while money will be required in Washington—This effectually quills [*sic*] any feeble impulse that I might have to start at once.

So I will wait as near an approach to anxiety as anything I can get up, to hear whether there is any prospect of my earning any pay from the Smithsonian. Perhaps if I staid only a short time at Washington it would be better that I should go there early rather than late, For if I could get up steam while there I might get on such a pressure as would carry me on after I got home despite the brakes my laziness puts on. . . .

I wonder if it would be highly disgraceful on my part to drop Natural History entirely, (that is after doing what you needed on the northern collections) and turn money grubber? Guess so. I confess my aspirations and ambition are nearly all gone—I'm a pretty low order of an animal just now—There—confound it, that's all the good comes of *thinking*.[37]

Kennicott's mood could change quickly, however, and emotional lows alternated with hyperactivity. While organizing the museum collections at the Chicago Academy of Sciences in 1863 and 1864, Kennicott became especially animated.[38] A similar pattern had emerged in the Mackenzie River District. When Kennicott wrote Baird from the Hudson's Bay Company territories, he periodically described his melancholy and apathetic state of mind, as in this example: "I too am getting seriously troubled by the effect of this monotonous life upon my mind and dread getting this lethergic [*sic*] habit fixed upon me. I was always lazy enough, but I used never to lose all mental energy for nearly a year at a time as has been the case here."[39] In 1862, when contemplating another year in the north, he wrote: "I will confess that I would, on my own account, much rather go out as soon as possible—for I find this D——d apathy rendering me about half idiotic, and I'm getting alarmed lest it gets fixed upon me as a habit—or disease—not to be gotten rid of even when I leave this monotonous life. I was always lazy enough, but now I'm a regular *beau rien*."[40]

Kennicott's constitution was admittedly delicate, but his frailties were emotional rather than physical. Any physical ailments that Kennicott might have had disappeared miraculously while he was living at the Hudson's Bay Company's northern posts, and he often referred to his newfound physicality in letters home. He endured the deprivations of northern life without complaint and was himself surprised by his ability to withstand cold weather, long bouts of physical exertion, and a diet disproportionately rich in fat and proteins.[41] His inability to attend regular school as a youth and his mysterious illnesses as an adult were therefore most likely indicative of his mental health—and that did not improve over time. Between 1860 and 1862 Kennicott blamed his despondency and lack of initiative on the northern environment, specifically the climate, but letters written after his return home to Illinois contained passages remarkably similar to those in letters written earlier. When Kennicott discovered that warmer weather did not improve his state of mind, he became convinced that returning north would lift his spirits.

Kennicott was only half right. During the Russian American expedition, the debilitating apathy and despondency he had previously experienced reemerged. Like before, those moods alternated with periods of frenetic activity. Kennicott could become so excitable as to be incomprehensible, and he was variously described by his men—even Dall—as crazy, insane, disagreeable, whimsical, foolish, and duplicitous. His men did not understand or care why he changed their itineraries so frequently, and they blamed him for the tenuous position that they found themselves in during the winter of 1865–66.[42] In 1859 Kennicott's enthusiasm and excitement had translated into a drive and energy that made him a valuable member of Baird's collecting team; in Alaska he was unable to channel his energy into collecting, and his instability was his undoing. During the night of 13 May, he left his quarters, walked out the gates of the fort, and was found lying dead by the river early the next morning. Before Kennicott left, one of his men, Frank Ketchum, prevented him from taking a revolver with him, but no one rose to keep him company or to watch over him.[43]

Although official accounts of Kennicott's death reported that he died of heart disease, many years later George Adams wrote that the whole camp believed that Kennicott had committed suicide by taking strychnine.[44] Kennicott's body was found less than five hours after he was last seen alive, and the description of the body—already rigid, with the arms folded across the chest—certainly provides circumstantial evidence in support of Adams's story.[45] Because death by strychnine poisoning is one of the few instances in which instant rigor mortis sets in,[46] and because the onset and completion of rigor mortis is retarded by cool temperatures like those typical of an Alaskan night in May, Adams's account seems plausible. Kennicott's body was found in an advanced, rather than preliminary, stage of rigor mortis, and that should not have been the case, given the climate and the short period of time that had elapsed between his being seen alive and his body's being found by his co-workers.

As a naturalist, Kennicott would have been aware of the horrible death produced by strychnine. He could have taken it only in a desperate, irrational moment. In any case, Dall's contention that Kennicott died of "disease of the heart on a desolate northern beach, alone," was undoubtedly correct. Dall continued: "He was murdered; not by the merciful knife but by a slow torture of the mind. By ungrateful subordinates, by an egotistic and selfish commander, by anxiety to fulfill his commands."[47] In the quaint and euphemistic phraseology of the Victorian period, Dall was saying that Kennicott had died of a broken heart.

CONCLUSION

An unprecedented number of specimens went to the Smithsonian as a result of Kennicott's visit to the Mackenzie River District between 1859 and 1862. Kennicott's successes in the Hudson's Bay Company territories admittedly reflected corporate support from an organization that had a well-established infrastructure, with stable socioeconomic relations and a fairly efficient system of communications and transportation, but the 1859 expedition also reflected the benefits of the methodological reorientation taking place in the natural sciences at midcentury. Between 1850 and 1870, data collecting was systematized and rationalized by scientists like Baird who were determined to define the empirical foundations of scientific inquiry. Taxonomic and systematic research, as well as the creation of a comprehensive research and public facility like the Smithsonian, required large collections, but the idiosyncratic and whimsical nature of collections acquired through an uncoordinated system of private donations could not serve as a reliable or comprehensive basis for serious scholarly work. Baird recognized that collections had to reflect research and institutional needs, and he attempted to make collections satisfy those needs by drafting and distributing instructions for collecting and observing in the field.

Kennicott went north with Baird's instructions. Because the Hudson's Bay Company endorsed Smithsonian science, including Baird's improved data gathering techniques, more specimens and data were sent from Rupert's Land to the Smithsonian between 1859 and 1867 than had ever left Hudson's Bay for European destinations. But the Mackenzie River collections were distinguished qualitatively as well as quantitatively. Specimens of several hundred zoological species were sent from the subarctic. Admittedly, their physical condition often suffered as a result of a lengthy and precarious journey or shortages of preservatives and packing materials, but the specimens nevertheless illustrated the diversity of fauna inhabiting northern ecosystems more comprehensively than ever before. Additionally, the documentation necessary for scientific studies of geographical distribution and speciation, as well as that needed for identifications based on morphological criteria, accompanied the specimens sent to the Smithsonian.

Similarly, the anthropological artifacts and ethnographies sent south by Hudson's Bay Company collectors were instrumental in the development of the modern social sciences, specifically in the application of an evolutionary paradigm to cultural studies and in the formalization of the methodology and motives for ethnographic research. Although commentaries on exotic cultures were a well-established component of travel literature, by 1860 ethnologists were identifying and distinguishing their approaches from earlier ones, carving a niche for ethnology as a science. They were distancing modern cultural studies from pre-modern studies that had their roots in literature and the humanities. Specimens of indigenous northern culture were crucial to that development.

The field notes, specimens, and ethnographies submitted by the Mackenzie River collectors also attest to the aptitude that the Hudson's Bay Company traders and northern native peoples had for fieldwork. The theoretical nature of science was perhaps never fully understood by either trader or trapper, but science as a purposeful and learned activity was easily integrated within both European and native cultural complexes.[1] Science was rarely an abstraction to the Mackenzie River collectors. They were workers, not theorists, but their importance should not be minimized. Anthropological artifacts were acquired according to prescribed techniques, and northern collectors carefully captured and pre-served zoological specimens. The Smithsonian was happy to receive those specimens; its scientists were gratified that their inducements had been sufficiently attractive and that their instructions not only had been appropriate but also had been adhered to remarkably well.

Because I am interested in science as a form of work, this book has been as much an excursion into labor history as an exercise in the history of science. Analyses of the activities of Smithsonian scientists and fieldworkers in terms of national development, as expressions of the Victorian ethos, or as the product of increased leisure time or societal leveling did not seem to offer satisfactory explanations for either the activities or the rationale of the scientists and collectors. For example, although it has been argued that Baird was instrumental in the purchase of Alaska, because Smith-sonian data were given to pro-purchase politicians,[2] the argument that Smithsonian science was the handmaiden of manifest destiny in the 1860s cannot be substantiated on the basis of the empirical data deposited at the Institution before the spring of 1867.

Even though Baird and Dall asserted that they had provided the data enabling members of the United States government to hold an informed debate on the merits of Russian America, such was simply not the case.[3] Little information would have been available as a result of Smithsonian explorations in the far north before 1867. The journals and notes kept by Kennicott were referred to at the government hearings into the purchase of Alaska, but his travels into Russian territories were extremely limited. He had been to Fort Yukon in 1861 before leaving the Hudson's Bay Company territories, and he had been approximately 200 miles inland from St. Michael's Redoubt in 1865. His journals and correspon-dence, though interesting, provided a far-from-comprehensive account of Alaska. Kennicott recorded information on the geography of the Nulato area because he was looking for a pass inland through the mountains, but he was unsuccessful in that endeavor and what he wrote about Alaskan climate and geography was not very positive.[4] He was much better versed in the geography, cli-mate, and resource base of the area around Fort Yukon, but he declined to divulge what he knew to Western Union in 1865.[5] By the time the government was collecting information on Alaska, he was dead.

Indeed, Senator Charles Sumner's lengthy speech in favor of the purchase of Russian America attested to the paucity of information available. The speech was long-winded and vague, exhibiting Sumner's ability to generalize from a skimpy factual basis. The senator offered his audience little concrete data about Alaska, and most of what he said came from secondary sources, not from first-hand observation by American scientists.[6] Much of the far North-west was still unknown in 1867, even to the Russian American and Hudson's Bay companies.[7] Only later expeditions would supply the data that could have won the support of individuals who were dubious about the wisdom of spending so much on such distant lands. Although William Healey Dall stayed on in the north to collect data until August 1868, he spent most of that time near St. Michael's, going to Fort Yukon only in the spring of 1868.[8] By autumn he was back on the coast. Dall's important inland collec-tions were made later, in conjunction with the United States Coast Survey and the Geological Survey.[9] Real progress in the exploration of Alaska was made between 1870 and 1885, only after $7.2 million had changed hands. Nor were the later findings as positive as those supposedly based on Smithsonian data and offered to congression-al representatives by Sumner and William Seward.[10]

Although taking credit for supplying data that the Smith-sonian did not yet really possess seems out of character for an upstanding empiricist such as Baird, any public acknowledgment or reference to Smithsonian work by Sumner and Seward might have translated into increased funding when the Institution made its annual bid for government support.[11] My examination of Baird's relationship with northern collectors certainly demon-strates that he was not above sycophancy to get specimens for his beloved Institution, and it would not have been out of character for him to have used the same tactic with Congress. Baird was a politician and a lobbyist, but his politics were Smithsonian poli-tics and his special interest was the advancement of Smithsonian science. He was neither an imperialist nor an expansionist, except perhaps insofar as those terms apply to curatorial acquisitiveness; to the advancement of scientific interests, broadly defined; and to the advancement of institutional interests, narrowly defined (as Smithsonian interests).

The types of data usually used to buttress political or territorial expansion were collected in reference to Baird's other research. Baird was interested in northern geography and climate only as they related to zoological systematics; he was not particularly interested in obtaining information on northern geology. Although any kind of natural history specimen was a welcome addition to the Smithsonian collections (including plants, fossils, soils, embryos, and microorganisms), during the 1860s Baird was preoccupied with birds and eggs. Taxonomic and systematic imperatives, rather than political ones, fueled Baird's interest in the north. He wanted northern natural history specimens, specifically ornithological and oological specimens, and would do whatever was necessary to get them.

Debates over whether volunteer, amateur, or noncareer field-workers took up science as a recreational pastime, as an intellectual avocation, or as their Christian duty are similarly tangential to my examination of Smithsonian fieldwork. They are also misleading. All three arguments were advanced as explanations for the scientific avocations of the Mackenzie River trader-collectors, but those men had additional reasons for becoming fieldworkers. The prestige of a quasi-professional affiliation with the Smithsonian was attractive to them. Furthermore, the trader-collectors did only a fraction of the work involved in collecting and forwarding scientific specimens. Many hands were needed to collect, sort, skin, stuff, and pack the specimens necessary to realize Baird's dream of making the Smithsonian the preeminent repository of North American natural history; native collectors performed most of those tasks.

Native classificatory schemes were largely irrelevant to Smithsonian science, because non-Western taxonomic systems that included mythical beings identified by their human ancestry or animistic powers were viewed as superstitions or worse. Nevertheless, indigenous collectors were a convenient and reliable labor pool. Indeed, the contributions of Athapaskan and Inuit collectors were crucial to Smithsonian research and museology, although the contributions were often dismissed as insignificant. Native collectors worked in cooperation with the Hudson's Bay Company men

CONCLUSION

whose donations were recognized repeatedly in the Smithsonian Institution's annual reports. It is true that some Hudson's Bay Company trader-collectors capitalized on native hardship when developing their collections, and that the most celebrated northern collectors misused native workers and misrepresented native labor as their own when assembling their collections, but native people were willing to adopt new occupations, irrespective of the transgressions of others, when the interests of outsiders seemed to coincide with their own. Native people were, and continue to be, depicted as incapable or unwilling to accommodate and accept elements of non-native society—except as hunters and trappers in the fur and provisioning trades—but northern Athapaskans and Inuit quickly integrated scientific work into existing economies. They did so, in fact, with a facility that often surprised southerners like Kennicott who viewed them as primitive and savage.

The contributions made by northern native people to Smithsonian science not only contradict assumptions about the inherent unsuitability of native people for civilized pursuits but also challenge historical interpretations that do little more than accept such assumptions uncritically. Native contributions do not, however, reflect a democratization of the sciences. The democratization that so many scholars have described as characteristic of the sciences during the nineteenth century is an explanatory concept that is of limited use here. Its use is limited precisely because so much of the actual fieldwork was done by native collectors. In analyzing Indian and Inuit participation in the Smithsonian scientific community, I discovered more about how the capitalist labor market functioned within the scientific community than I learned about the dissemination or operation of democratic principles. Admittedly, Baird fostered increased participation in the sciences, and he did make the empirical sciences accessible to individuals with little or no knowledge of Western science, but his methodological innovations also reflected the scientific community's needs. There would have been scant support for the recruitment of indigenous collectors if it had not been in the interests of the scientific community to recruit and train on-site. Indigenous populations could provide a cheap, efficient, and reliable corps of fieldworkers whether they adopted the scientific ethos or not.

Alternatively, Smithsonian scientists, largely through Kennicott, had to convince northerners that doing fieldwork could be useful to them. The Mackenzie River collectors would have had slight interest in the Smithsonian's collecting program if Baird's incentives had been inadequate or inappropriate. Social status, prestige, recognition among scientists, and Baird's appreciation rewarded the better-educated collectors such as Bernard Rogan Ross, Roderick Ross MacFarlane, James Lockhart, and George Barnston. But even such sophisticated collectors were susceptible to the inducements of consumer goods, especially alcohol and books.

The benefits of the socioeconomic relationship that was established between Smithsonian scientists and the Mackenzie River collectors were made abundantly clear during Kennicott's 1865–66 expedition to Alaska. Smithsonian successes in the Hudson's Bay Company territories stand out markedly in comparison with the poor collections made later in the adjacent territory. The difference between success and failure rested, to a large extent, on an ability to persuade individuals to work for science. Although the first obstacle to recruiting indigenous Alaskan collectors was an inability to communicate with either the Russians or the Alaskan native peoples, members of the telegraphic expedition were also less than eager to collect natural history specimens. Those men, although civilians, were given military commissions; they were quite satisfied with their improved social position as lieutenants. Disaffection with their status translated into squabbles over promotions within the new and rather unstable paramilitary structure of the Western Union expedition, not into scientific work. Aside from Dall's marine collections, the specimens submitted by Western Union's scientific corps between 1865 and 1868 were notably unexceptional, given the time and money invested by both the company and the Smithsonian and given that Baird's new collecting program had already been tested and proved successful in the Mackenzie River District.

Although some of the Mackenzie River collectors conformed ostensibly to the image of the gentleman-scientist—keeping cabinets; dabbling in taxonomy, systematics, and anthropology; and writing articles for scientific journals—they were part of a network organized around, and benefiting, the Smithsonian. Their contributions were empirical and functional rather than theoretical or inventive. Baird admittedly enticed and encouraged educated northerners into collecting by corresponding with them on a regular basis, by sending gifts, and by welcoming them into an elite socio-intellectual group, but even the best-educated and most sophisticated of the northern collectors were at the bottom of the hierarchy developing around the Smithsonian and the North American scientific community. They were field*workers*. In 1865, no such pool of collectors existed in Russian America. Ironically, the failure of the Western Union expedition as a source of specimens, despite Baird's and Kennicott's best efforts, confirmed what had already been demonstrated in Mackenzie River. Fieldwork on the scale envisioned by Baird was more than a genteel hobby. It was indeed work.

APPENDIX: THE MACKENZIE RIVER
COLLECTIONS, 1859–1871

Nineteenth-century record keeping techniques were inadequate to cope with the volume of specimens arriving at the Smithsonian. The accession records of the Smithsonian Institution permit only an approximation of the sum total of its collections. It is similarly difficult to determine the precise number of specimens sent south by the Hudson's Bay Company collectors. Smithsonian registration numbers, for example, often indicated the kind rather than the quantity of specimens. In 1865 Baird calculated that each registration number represented approximately five specimens.[1] Individual entries in the accession records of the U.S. National Museum often covered several different specimens, and oological specimens, the most highly prized northern acquisitions, were particularly susceptible to exclusion from the registers.[2] Parent birds were assigned numbers in the registers, but the presence of eggs was often simply noted with the descriptive remarks that accompanied the ornithological specimens.

It is also impossible to be sure that the specimens entered under an individual's name were, in fact, collected and prepared by that person. Correspondence between northern collectors and Smithsonian scientists indicates that some collectors indiscriminantly registered—as their own—specimens collected by both native people and their fellow traders. Moreover, although several sources have been used to determine the number of specimens sent south from the Mackenzie River District, even together they do not provide a comprehensive account of specimens submitted. In only 2 of the 13 years in which specimens were sent out of the north are the data anything but inconclusive. In 1870 no specimens were sent south, and in 1871 the Smithsonian received its last Mackenzie River specimen from MacFarlane.[3] The table presented here is therefore intended to demonstrate the relative rather than the absolute levels of activity of the collectors officially credited with sending specimens from the Mackenzie River District to the Smithsonian Institution.[4]

Mackenzie River Specimens Submitted to the Smithsonian Institution

Submitter	Year											Total	Approximate % of total
	1859	1860	1861	1862	1863	1864	1865	1866	1867	1868	1869		
R. R. MacFarlane		8	62	550	1,000	1,520	1,830	463	97	6	179	5,715	48
B. R. Ross		840	502	774	Some			138	1	4		>2,259	19
R. Kennicott	208	572	428		47	30		62	23			1,370	11.5
J. Lockhart		78	4	980	Some	67	Some	1	1			>1,131	9.5
S. Jones				76			Some		525			>601	5
C. P. Gaudet			2		Some		133	45	1			>181	1.5
J. Reid		102	41		Some							>143	1
A. Mackenzie		142	1									143	1
W. L. Hardisty		Some	55		Some				8			>63	0.5
A. Flett			1		57							58	0.5
W. Brass		7			36							43	0.5
J. Flett		35	Some	6	Some		Some					>41	<0.5
J. S. Onion		27	Some		Some							>27	<0.5
N. Taylor		11	10									21	<0.5
J. Sibbeston					21							21	<0.5
A. Hoole				10								10	<0.1
Mrs. C. Ross		1	6									7	<0.1
J. Dunlop		6										6	0.1
L. Clarke		Some	Some		Some							Some	?
R. Campbell		Some	Some									Some	?
Mrs. Hardisty		Some										Some	?
T. Swanston		Some										Some	?
W. W. Kirkby		Some										Some	?
Others		43		4						1 + some		>48	≈0.5
Total	208	>1,872	>1,112	2,400	>1,161	1,617	>1,963	709	>657	10	179	>11,888	

ABBREVIATIONS

BCA — British Columbia Archives, Victoria

BDAS — Biographical Dictionary of American Science: The Seventeenth through the Nineteenth Centuries, ed. Clark A. Elliott (Westport, Conn.: Greenwood Press, 1979)

DCB — Dictionary of Canadian Biography (Toronto: University of Toronto Press, 1966–)

HBC — Hudson's Bay Company

HBCA — Hudson's Bay Company Archives

HBC Corr. Coll. — Hudson's Bay Company Correspondence Collection, Washington, D.C.

NMNH — U.S. National Museum of Natural History, Washington, D.C.

Pacific Railroad Survey Reports — Reports of Explorations and Surveys, to Ascertain the Most Practicable and Economical Route for a Railroad from the Mississippi River to the Pacific Ocean

PAM — Provincial Archives of Manitoba, Winnipeg

RU — Record Unit

SIA — Smithsonian Institution Archives, Washington, D.C.

SIAR — Annual Report of the Board of Regents of the Smithsonian Institution (Washington, D.C.)

ABBREVIATIONS

Smithsonian Contr. Knowl. — Smithsonian Contributions to Knowledge (Washington, D.C.)

Smithsonian Misc. Coll. — Smithsonian Miscellaneous Collections (Washington, D.C.)

NOTES

PREFACE AND ACKNOWLEDGMENTS

1. Nathan Reingold, ed., *Science in Nineteenth-Century America: A Documentary History* (New York: Hill and Wang, 1964), 153, contends that the Smithsonian had "acquired the status of a venerable symbol" in nineteenth-century American society, but he attributes that accomplishment to Joseph Henry rather than to Baird. Henry believed that his work in the physical sciences was more scientific than the work of natural scientists such as Baird, and Reingold concurs with Henry. Moreover, although Reingold's assessment of the Smithsonian museum as the "nation's attic" is perhaps correct for a later period in the Institution's history, the earlier history of the museum and the Natural History Department is not so clear-cut. The processes of collection, preservation, identification, and classification of zoological, botanical, geological, and ethnological specimens contributed to contemporary perceptions of the Smithsonian as the symbol of American science as much as the Institution's laboratory experiments and prestigious publications did.

INTRODUCTION

1. Biographical information on Baird comes from a variety of sources, including the following: George Brown Goode, "The Three Secretaries," in *The Smithsonian Institution, 1846–1896: The History of Its First Half Century,* ed. G. B. Goode (Washington, D.C.: Devine Press, 1897), 115–234; William Healey Dall, *Spencer Fullerton Baird: A Biography* (Philadelphia: J. B. Lippincott, 1915) and

"Professor Baird in Science," SIAR 1888, 731–38; Garrick Mallery, "Relations between Professor Baird and Participating Societies," SIAR 1888, 717–20; John Wesley Powell, "Personal Characteristics of Professor Baird," SIAR 1888, 739–44; Robert Ridgway, "Spencer Fullerton Baird," SIAR 1888, 703–13; William B. Taylor, "Professor Baird as Administrator," SIAR 1888, 721–29; Elmer Charles Herber, "Spencer F. Baird—World Famous Naturalist," in *John and Mary's College,* Boyd Lee Spahr Lectures in Americana, 1951–1956, Dickinson College (Carlisle, Pa.: Fleming H. Revell, 1956); E. C. Herber, ed., *Correspondence between Spencer Fullerton Baird and Louis Agassiz—Two Pioneer American Naturalists* (Washington, D.C.: Smithsonian Institution, 1963); Wilcomb E. Washburn, "Joseph Henry's Conception of the Purpose of the Smithsonian Institution," in *A Cabinet of Curiosities: Five Episodes in the Evolution of American Museums,* ed. Walter Muir Whitehill (Charlottesville: University Press of Virginia, 1967), 106–66; William A. Deiss, "Spencer F. Baird and His Collectors," *Journal of the Society for the Bibliography of Natural History* 9, no. 4 (1980): 635–45, and "The Making of a Naturalist: Spencer F. Baird, the Early Years," in *From Linnaeus to Darwin: Commentaries on the History of Biology and Geology* (London: Society for the History of Natural History, 1985), 141–48. Baird specifically referred to his scholarly background in his letter of application for the Smithsonian position; see Baird to Joseph Henry, 25 Feb. 1847, reprinted in Dall, *Baird,* 158–60.

2. See W. H. Dall, "List of Works Containing Information in Regards to Alaska and the Adjacent Territories," Appendix H in *Alaska and Its Resources* (Boston, 1870), 595–609.

3. Lawson, *Description and Natural History of North Carolina* (1700–1730); Catesby, *The Natural History of Carolina, Florida, Etc.* (1731; 1743; 1748); Edwards, *Natural History of Uncommon Birds* (1751); Forster, *A Catalogue of the Animals of North America* (1771); Kalm, *Travels into North America, Containing Its Natural History . . .* (1770); Pennant, *Arctic Zoology* (1784–85).

4. Wilson, *American Ornithology; or, The Natural History of the Birds of the United States* (1808–14); Bonaparte, *American Ornithology; or, The Natural History of Birds Inhabiting the United States, Not Given by Wilson* (1825–33); Audubon, *The Birds of America* (1840–44); Nuttall, *A Manual of the Ornithology of the United States and Canada* (1832).

5. Audubon and Bachman, *The Viviparous Quadrupeds of North America* (1842–59); Harlan, *Fauna Americana* (1825).

6. Say, *American Entomology* (1824–28) and *American Conchology* (1830–34); Holbrook, *North American Herpetology* (1836–38).

7. Seemann, *Botany of the H.M.S. Herald, 1852–1857;* Bongard, *Observations sur la vegetation d l'île de Sitka* (1831); Michaux, *The North American Sylva* (1810–13); Nuttall, *The Genera of North American Plants, and a Catalogue of the Species to the Year 1817* (1818); Eaton, *Manual of Botany for North America* (1829); Beck, *Botany of the Northern and Middle States* (1833); Torrey, appendix to John Lindley, *An Introduction to the Natural System of Botany* (1831); Gray with Torrey, *A Flora of North America* (1838–43).

8. Also important was Richardson's *Botany of Captain Beechey's Voyage* (1841).

9. Richardson noted the sources of his specimens and credited collectors who had made his publication possible; Hooker did the same. John Richardson, William Swainson, and Rev. William Kirby, *Fauna Boreali-Americana; or, The Zoology of the Northern Parts of British America, Containing Descriptions of the Objects of Natural History Collected on the Late Northern Land Expeditions, Under Command of Captain Sir John Franklin,* 3 vols., pt. 1—*The Quadrupeds,* pt. 2—*Birds,* pt. 3—*Fishes* (London: John Murray, 1829-36), 1:xiv-xix. William Jackson Hooker, *Flora Boreali-Americana; or, The Botany of the Northern Parts of British America, Compiled Principally from the Plants Collected by Dr. Richardson & Mr. Drummond on the late northern Expeditions, Under Command of Captain Sir John Franklin, R.N. To Which are added (by permission of the Horticultural Society of London,) Those of Mr. Douglas, from North-West America, And of Other Naturalists* (1833-40; reprint, New York: Hafner, 1960).

10. Information on the Hudson's Bay Company contributions can be found in *Fauna Boreali-Americana,* 1:xix, 3:x; information on the museum collections used by Richardson can be found in *Fauna Boreali-Americana,* 2:xii.

11. S. F. Baird, Thomas Mayo Brewer, and R. Ridgway, *A History of North American Birds: Land Birds,* 3 vols. (1874; reprint, Boston: Little, Brown, 1905), 1:vi.

12. Hubert Howe Bancroft, *History of Alaska, 1730-1885* (1886; reprint, New York: Antiquarian Press, 1960). See also James Wickersham, *A Bibliography of Alaskan Literature, 1724-1924,* Miscellaneous Publications of the Alaska Agricultural College and School of Mines (Cordova, Alaska: Cordova Daily Times Print, 1927).

13. SIAR 1850, 46-48.

14. Good working definitions of systematics and taxonomy are provided by G. G. Simpson: "Systematics is the scientific study of the kinds and diversity of organisms and of any and all relationships among them" and "[Taxonomy is the . . .] theoretical study of classification, including its bases, principles, procedures and rules" (*Principles of Animal Taxonomy* [New York: Columbia University Press, 1961], 7, 11.

15. Theodore Gill, "Zoology," in *Smithsonian Institution,* ed. Goode, 717.

16. S. F. Baird and Charles Girard, *Catalogue of North American Reptiles in the Museum of the Smithsonian Institution,* pt. 1, *Serpents* (Washington, D.C.: Smithsonian Institution, 1853); SIAR 1853, 52; SIAR 1856, 60.

17. S. F. Baird to William Baird, 25 May 1846; Joseph Henry to S. F. Baird, 24 Apr. 1850, in Dall, *Baird,* 136-37, 209-10. "Circular to Any Officer of the Army," regarding specimen collection for Spencer F. Baird from S. Churchill, 6 Aug. 1850, SIA, RU 7002, Box 39.

18. Supporting Henry's nomination for secretary were Alexander Bache, one of the first regents of the Institution; Michael Faraday, the discoverer of the law of electromagnetic induction; and Benjamin Silliman, a prominent North American scientist. See Joel Orosz, "Curators and Culture: An Interpretive History of the Museum Movement in America, 1773-1870" (Ph.D. diss., Case Western Reserve University, 1986), 271.

19. Washburn, "Joseph Henry's Conception," provides a balanced discussion of Henry's view of collections and museums. Curtis M. Hinsley, Jr., *Savages and Scientists: The Smithsonian Institution and the Development of American Anthropology, 1846–1910* (Washington, D.C.: Smithsonian Institution Press, 1981), also provides a sympathetic interpretation of Henry's anti-museum stance. For more on Henry's views on natural history collections and museology, see Henry's reports to Congress, SIAR 1851–62.

20. Orosz, "Curators and Culture," 2.

21. Henry to Baird, 23, 24 Apr. 1850, in Dall, *Baird,* 207–9, 209–10.

22. Baird to Henry, 3 Nov. 1849; Henry to Baird, 23, 24 Apr., 28 May 1850, in Dall, *Baird,* 190–93, 207–9, 209–10, 210–11.

23. Dall, *Baird,* 229–39; Remington Kellogg, "A Century of Progress in Smithsonian Biology," *Science* 104, no. 2693 (1946), 133.

24. SIAR 1867, 76–78.

25. The Smithsonian's annual reports enumerated cumulative accessions periodically. The first attempt to analyze the collections statistically was made in 1858, but a numerical breakdown of the collections appeared every second year for the next 20 years. In the following list, the total number of specimens registered at the Smithsonian is given after the date, although the source of the information is not always that year's report: 1851—911; 1852—1,188; 1853—1,388; 1854—4,979; 1855—7,675; 1856—11,222; 1857—16,158; 1858—25,506; 1859—37,197; 1860—55,389; 1861—66,075; 1862—74,764; 1863—85,726; 1864—95,922; 1865—111,847; 1866—119,101. SIAR 1858, 57; 1860, 73; 1862, 57; 1864, 84; 1865, 84; 1866, 45.

26. George Daniels, *Science in American Society: A Social History* (New York: Alfred A. Knopf, 1971), 267–69, contends that the Civil War allowed scientists to wrest control of American science from politicians, who were otherwise occupied. An examination of the Smithsonian Institution during the war years tends to support Daniels's thesis; see also "The Smithsonian, Seedbed of Science," in Robert V. Bruce, *The Launching of Modern American Science, 1846–1876* (New York: Alfred A. Knopf, 1987), 187–200.

27. The details of Kennicott's northern travels may be found in several places, including the Smithsonian annual reports, especially SIAR 1859, 66, and are described more fully in Edward A. Preble, "A Biological Investigation of the Athabaska-Mackenzie Region," *North American Fauna,* no. 27, U.S. Department of Agriculture (Washington, D.C.: Government Printing Office, 1908), 70–71. See also Kennicott's correspondence with Baird in the Spencer Fullerton Baird Papers, 1833–89, Incoming Correspondence, Box 27, RU 7002, SIA, and in the Robert Kennicott Papers, Box 13, RU 7215, SIA; "Journal of Robert Kennicott, May 19, 1859–February 11, 1862," reprinted in *The First Scientific Exploration of Russian America and the Purchase of Alaska,* ed. James Alton James (Chicago: Northwestern University, 1942), 46–135, and James's introduction, 7–10. References to Kennicott's travels are made in Greg Thomas, "The Smithsonian and the Hudson's Bay Company," *Prairie Forum* 10, no. 2 (1985): 285; K. S. Coates, "The Kennicott Network: Robert Kennicott and the Far Northwest," in *Proceed-*

ings of the Yukon Museums and Historical Association (1982); and two earlier articles—H. Collins, "Wilderness Exploration and Alaska's Purchase," *Living Wilderness* (Dec. 1946), and H. G. Deignan, "The HBC and the Smithsonian," *The Beaver* (June 1947).

28. In 1670 the English fur trade merchants who organized themselves into the Hudson's Bay Company claimed much of North America as their own. They named this new territory in honor of the first governor of the company—Prince Rupert.

29. B. R. Ross, "List of Species Collected at Fort Simpson, 1860 and 1861," Anderson Papers, HBCA, PAM, E.37/13. Also "Collected Notes, Lists, and Catalogs on Birds," SIA, RU 7215, Box 13, Robert Kennicott; Box 29, Folder: Bernard R. Ross; Box 14, Roderick Ross MacFarlane; Box 13, S. Jones; Box 9, Charles P. Gaudet. Information on Gaudet's collection is also found in Gaudet to Baird, 17 July 1862, SIA, HBC Corr. Coll., Folder 18. Information on specimens submitted is also found in L. Clarke to Baird, 1 Dec. 1862, SIA, HBC Corr. Coll., Folder 9. Official Smithsonian records are contained in Accession Records, Office of the Registrar, U.S. National Museum, RU 699T, or on microfilm (RU 305). The reports of the assistant secretary, SIAR 1857–66, also contain data on northern specimens. A tabular presentation of the data is given in the Appendix of this book.

30. For example, the arctic collections received in 1863 (including some specimens from 1862) filled 40 boxes and packages, weighing approximately 3,000 pounds (SIAR 1863, 53). The collections received in 1864 filled 29 cases (SIAR 1864, 81), and in 1865 the "usual" number of cases (30) of specimens were sent (W. L. Hardisty to Baird, 4 Aug. 1865, SIA, HBC Corr. Coll., Folder 22). Forty-nine cases of specimens were shipped to the Smithsonian from Fort Garry in 1866. The first 33, shipped in June, weighed 2,096 pounds (James R. Clare to Baird, 6 June, 4 Sept. 1866, SIA, HBC Corr. Coll., Folder 8). Thirty cases of specimens were sent out of the district to the south in 1867, although they may not have reached Washington until 1868 (Thomas Hardisty to Baird, 20 Feb. 1868, SIA, HBC Corr. Coll., Folder 21). Sixteen boxes, 11 packages, and 1 keg were received from MacFarlane alone in 1868 (SIAR 1868, 57).

31. E. A. Preble, "A Biological Investigation of the Hudson Bay Region," *North American Fauna*, no. 22, Department of Agriculture, Division of Biological Survey (Washington, D.C.: Government Printing Office, 1902), 24–26.

32. Susan Stewart, "George Simpson: Collector," *The Beaver* (Summer 1982): 4–9.

33. Dall, "Professor Baird," 735.

34. Ridgway, "Baird," 706.

35. The northern specimens were presumably culled from those that had been collected by Sir John Richardson and then later deposited in the British Museum by Joseph Sabine, who was noteworthy for his position as the honorary secretary of the Horticultural Society. For details of the British donation, see SIAR 1857, 48. For details of Sabine's involvement in the disposition of Richardson's specimens, see *Arctic Ordeal: The Journal of John Richardson, Surgeon-Naturalist*

with Franklin, 1820–1822, ed. C. Stuart Houston (Kingston and Montreal: McGill-Queen's University Press, 1984), 198.

36. SIAR 1854, 92; 1856, 53; 1857, 46; 1858, 50; 1859, 64; 1877, 106.

CHAPTER 1

1. SIAR 1855, 31.
2. SIAR 1850, 45.
3. Baird to Henry, 3 Nov. 1849, in Dall, *Baird,* 190–93.
4. SIAR 1865, 41; S. F. Baird, *Catalogue of North American Birds, Chiefly in the Museum of the Smithsonian Institution* (1859, reissued in 1862 [in Smithsonian Misc. Coll., vol. 2]; reprinted from vol. 9 of *Pacific Railroad Survey Reports,* by S. F. Baird, John Cassin, and George N. Lawrence [1858]) and *Review of North American Birds in the Museum of the Smithsonian Institution,* pt. 1, *North and Middle America* (Washington, D.C.: Smithsonian Institution, 1864–66).
5. S. F. Baird, T. M. Brewer, and R. Ridgway, *The Water Birds of North America* (Boston: Little, Brown, 1884) and *History of North American Birds.* For reprints of Baird's articles ("Notes on a Collection of Birds Made by Mr. John Xantus, at Cape St. Lucas, Lower California, and Now in the Museum of the Smithsonian Institution," *Proceedings of the Academy of Natural Sciences of Philadelphia* 11 [1859], and "The Distribution and Migrations of North American Birds," *American Journal of Science and Arts* 41 [1866]), see *American Natural History Studies: The Bairdian Period,* ed. Keir B. Sterling (New York: Arno Press, 1974).
6. S. F. Baird, "Catalogue of Birds Found in the Neighborhood of Carlisle, Cumberland County, Pa.," in *The Centennial Check-list of the Birds of Cumberland County, Pennsylvania, and Her Borders, 1840–1843,* by Edward Snively Frey (Lemoyne, Pa.: E. S. Frey, 1843); "Catalogue of Birds Found in the Neighborhood of Carlisle, Cumberland County, Pa.," in *The Centennial Check-list of the Birds of Cumberland County, Pennsylvania, and Her Borders, 1845,* by E. S. Frey (1845); "Contributions towards a Catalogue of the Trees and Shrubs of Cumberland County, Pa.," *Literary Record and Journal of the Linnaean Association of Pennsylvania College* (1845): 57–63; "Revision of the North American Tailed-Batrachia, with Descriptions of New Genera and Species," *Journal of the Academy of Natural Sciences in Philadelphia* 2d ser., 1 (Oct. 1849); *Hints for Preserving Objects of Natural History* (Carlisle, Pa.: Gitt and Hinckley, 1846).
7. Deiss, "Making of a Naturalist," 141–48, and "Baird and His Collectors," 637.
8. The best study of the intellectual and methodological development of the life sciences is Ernst Mayr, *The Growth of Biological Thought: Diversity, Evolution, and Inheritance* (Cambridge: Belknap Press, Harvard University Press, 1982). Mayr's work has been invaluable to my understanding of the natural sciences in North America and of the development of the natural sciences generally. See also E. L. Kessel, ed., *A Century of Progress in the Natural Sciences, 1853–1953* (San Francisco: California Academy of Sciences, 1955).

9. Goode, "Three Secretaries," 172–73.

10. For a reference to the Baird-Agassiz dispute over the catalogue, see introduction to Herber, *Correspondence,* 12. See also the following letters reprinted in the same book for specific information on the dispute: Agassiz to Baird, 27 June, 5 July 1853, 54–56, 60–61; Baird to Agassiz, 30 June 1853, 56–60.

11. Baird to Agassiz, 30 June 1853, in Herber, *Correspondence,* 56–60.

12. Ibid., Agassiz to Baird, 27 June 1853, 55–56.

13. Louis Agassiz, "Essay on Classification," from *Contributions to the Natural History of the United States of America* (1857), reprinted in *The Intelligence of Louis Agassiz: A Specimen Book of Scientific Writings,* ed. Guy Davenport (Boston: Beacon Press, 1963), 67–69.

14. Baird to Agassiz, 30 June 1853, in Herber, *Correspondence,* 58.

15. See S. F. Baird, *Catalogue of North American Mammals, Chiefly in the Museum of the Smithsonian Institution* (1857; reprinted from vol. 8 of *Pacific Railroad Survey Reports*), xv, and *Catalogue of North American Birds* (1859), lvi. See also Dall, "Professor Baird," 732.

16. Taxonomic revision is undertaken either to clarify ordinal relationships or to expedite species identification. The first type of revision entails a complete reorganization of a classificatory system and expresses fundamental assumptions about the relationships within and between classes. The second type of revision tends toward a multiplication of the numbers of families, genera, species, and subspecies to provide a comprehensive framework for identification. Most of Baird's revisions exemplify the latter case. For a discussion of the nature of taxonomic revisionism, see Herbert Friedmann, "Recent Revisions in Classification and Their Biological Significance," in *Recent Studies in Avian Biology,* ed. Albert Wolfson (Urbana: University of Illinois Press, 1955), 23–24. See also E. Mayr, "Macrotaxonomy: The Science of Classifying" and "Microtaxonomy: The Science of Species," in *Growth of Biological Thought,* 145–208, 251–97.

17. Information on Baird's contribution to mammalian classification can be found in *Catalogue of North American Mammals,* xviii–xxxiv. More specifically, Baird introduced the following genera in *Catalogue of North American Birds: Bucephala,* xxiii; *Pedioecetes,* xxi, liv; *Sphyrapicus,* xviii, xxviii, 80, 101; *Oreortyx,* xlv; *Heleroscelus,* xxii, xlvii, 728, 734; *Micropalama,* xxii, xlvii, 714, 726; *Stelgidopteryx,* xxxiv, 312; *Catherpes,* xix, xxvi, 354, 356; *Oreoscoptes,* xix, xxxv, 346; *Phainopepla,* xix, xxxiv, 923; *Protonotaria,* pxix, xxxi, 235, 239; *Oporornis,* xix, xxxii, 240, 246; *Melospiza,* xx, xl, 440, 476; *Rhynchophanes,* xx, xxxviii, 432. The following subgenera were added to the same catalogue: *Xenopicus,* xviii, xxviii, 83, 96; *Lanivireo,* xix, xxxv, 329; *Helospiza,* xx, xl, 476. Baird's subsequent publications also contained new species and classificatory divisions.

18. Mayr, *Growth of Biological Thought,* 213. See pp. 158–62 for a discussion of downward classification and pp. 190-95 for a discussion of upward classification.

19. Ibid., 192. Mayr also states: "[U]pward classification is possible only if one understands what one is grouping—that is, species. Thus, a prerequisite of the compositional approach was a knowledge of species, even if essentialistically defined" (pp. 192–93).

20. Erwin Stresemann, *Ornithology, from Aristotle to the Present* (Cambridge: Harvard University Press, 1975), 155–56; Elliott Coues, *Key to North American Birds* (1872; reprint, Boston: Page Co., 1903), xix–xx.

21. American Ornithologists' Union, *Check-list of North American Birds,* 5th ed. (Baltimore: Lord Baltimore Press, 1957), 621.

22. S. F. Baird, J. Cassin, and G. N. Lawrence, *The Birds of North America: The Descriptions of Species Based Chiefly on the Collections in the Museum of the Smithsonian Institution* (1860; reprint, New York: Arno Press, 1974), 463.

23. Josslyn Van Tyne and Andrew Berger, *Fundamentals of Ornithology,* 5th ed. (New York: Dover, 1971), 350.

24. On other reformers, see Stresemann, *Ornithology,* 264.

25. For a discussion of the historical precedents of the code, see introduction to *International Code of Zoological Nomenclature,* 3d ed., ed. W. D. L. Ride et al. (London: International Trust for Zoological Nomenclature, 1985), xv–xvi. See also Stresemann, *Ornithology,* 250–68, and Mayr, *Growth of Biological Thought,* 290–91.

26. Stresemann, *Ornithology,* 246.

27. Ibid.

28. For a discussion of the various systems spawned by the Strickland Code, see David Heppell, "The Evolution of the Code of Zoological Nomenclature," in *History in the Service of Systematics,* ed. Alwyne Wheeler and James H. Price (London: Society for the Bibliography of Natural History, 1981), 136–37. For a broader view of the international taxonomic debate, see Stresemann, *Ornithology,* 243–68.

29. An introduction to avian systematics can be found in Van Tyne and Berger, *Fundamentals of Ornithology,* 360–61. Stresemann, *Ornithology,* 243, 321–22, describes the historical context and content of early developments in ornithology and discusses Bergmann and Gloger. Baird's analyses are presented in "Notes on a Collection of Birds" and "Distribution and Migrations."

30. Alden H. Miller, "Concepts and Problems of Avian Systematics in Relation to Evolutionary Processes," in *Recent Studies in Avian Biology,* ed. Wolfson, 6–7.

31. Stresemann, *Ornithology,* 243–46, points out that the members of the Bairdian school, in particular, had a Lamarckian bias and that J. A. Allen, one of America's most famous nineteenth-century ornithologists and a member of the Bairdian school, was a self-proclaimed Lamarckian.

32. On J. A. Allen's impact on avian systematics, see Stresemann, *Ornithology,* 244–45; Olin Sewall Pettingill, *Ornithology in Laboratory and Field,* 5th ed. (New York: Academic Press, 1985), 111; and Van Tyne and Berger, *Fundamentals of Ornithology,* 359–60.

33. Baird, "Distribution and Migrations," 191. Dean Allard, "Baird, Spencer Fullerton," in *Dictionary of Scientific Biography,* ed. Charles Coulston Gillispie (New York: Charles Scribner's Sons, 1970), 405, has also noted Baird's particular view of the role that environment played in taxonomy, although he emphasizes the significance that Baird's paper on distribution and migration had as a manifestation of Darwinism in North America.

34. Baird, Brewer, and Ridgway, *History of North American Birds*, 3:112–20.

35. See Mayr, *Growth of Biological Thought*, 240.

36. On Allen, see Van Tyne and Berger, *Fundamentals of Ornithology*, 156–57. For an exposition of Baird's views on Sclater's zoogeography, see Baird, "Distribution and Migrations," 78–90.

37. SIAR 1851, 22; 1855, 14–15; 1858, 14–15; 1860, 74.

38. Kennicott to MacFarlane, 15 Apr. 1864, SIA, RU 7072.

39. S. F. Baird, "Instructions in Reference to Collecting Nests and Eggs of North American Birds," Smithsonian Misc. Coll., vol. 2, no. 139 (1862), 10.

40. Thomas Mayo Brewer, *North American Oology*, pt. 1, *Raptores and Fissirostres*, Smithsonian Contr. Knowl., vol. 11, no. 89 (1859), v; T. M. Brewer and S. F. Baird, "Circular in Reference to Collecting Nests and Eggs of North American Birds," Smithsonian Misc. Coll., vol. 2, no. 139 (1862), 6.

41. Information on the zoological and anthropological specimens submitted by northern collectors to the Smithsonian has been obtained from the following sources: "Index to Catalogue of Specimens" and "Packing Account and Recapitulation of Seven Cases of Natural History Specimens, 01 June 1862–20 September 1862," SIA, RU 7215, Box 29, Folder: B. R. Ross; "List of Specimens Collected at Great Slave Lake, 1868," SIA, RU 7215, Box 13, Strachan Jones; "List of Specimens of Natural History, 1865," SIA, RU 7215, Box 9, C. P. Gaudet; and Registers, Accession Records, Department of Anthropology, NMNH, vols. 1–3, SIA, RU 6990T, and Computer Printout, Ident. MNH4 122G113, MNH-ANN.

42. Registration numbers generally indicate taxon and type, rather than number of specimens. Baird calculated that each registration number represented approximately five specimens. SIAR 1862, 56.

43. Ridgway, "Baird," SIAR 1888, 709–10.

CHAPTER 2

1. SIAR 1850, 45.

2. Kennicott to MacFarlane, 29 Apr. 1863, SIA, RU 7072.

3. Baird's pamphlet of general directions for the collection and preservation of natural history specimens was initially prepared during 1850 (SIAR 1851, 50) and issued in the spring of 1851 (SIAR 1851, 45). After that, its contents were expanded, and a letter from the secretary of war, dated 17 January 1852, was attached. In that letter the secretary granted Smithsonian collectors free transportation for their specimens. A copy of the expanded circular is found in Smithsonian Misc. Coll., vol. 2, no. 34 (1862), 2–40. Specialized instructions were initially printed in SIAR 1858, as follows: T. M. Brewer, "Instructions in Reference to Collecting Nests and Eggs of North American Birds," 153–57; and a compilation entitled "Instructions for Collecting Insects" (including brief instructions for the collection of Hymenoptera, Orthoptera, Hemiptera, and Neuroptera, as well as more-comprehensive instructions—John LeConte's "Instructions for Collecting Coleoptera," Hermann Loew and Baron Carl Robert

Romanovich von der Osten Sacken's "Instructions for Collecting Diptera," and Brackinridge Clemens's "Instructions for Collecting Lepidoptera"), 158–200. The following was prepared in 1859: Isaac Lea, P. P. Carpenter, William Stimpson, W. G. Binney, and Temple Prime, "Circular in Reference to Collecting North American Shells" (SIAR 1859, 55). See also I. Lea et al., "Check-lists of the Shells of North America," Smithsonian Misc. Coll., vol. 2, no. 128 (1862).

4. SIAR 1863, 14.

5. Baird, "Directions for Collecting, Preserving, and Transporting Specimens of Natural History," Smithsonian Misc. Coll., vol. 2, no. 34 (1862), 5–6.

6. Ibid., J. Henry's introductory letter, 3.

7. Alfred Newton, "Suggestions for Forming Collections of Birds' Eggs," appendix to Brewer and Baird, "Circular in Reference to Collecting Nests and Eggs," 12.

8. For a definition of biometrics and a description of the methods associated with twentieth-century zoological statistics, see G. G. Simpson, A. Roe, and R. Lewontin, *Quantitative Zoology,* rev. ed. (New York: Harcourt, Brace, 1960). For a discussion of Baird's statistical techniques, see Miller, "Concepts and Problems," 7.

9. *BDAS,* 153–54, 196; SIAR 1859, 33. For lay terminology and scientific nomenclature of insects, see W. P. Pycraft, *The Standard Natural History: From Amoeba to Man* (New York: Frederick Warne, 1931), 194–345.

10. *BDAS,* 20–21.

11. John Woodward, *Brief Instructions for making observations in all Parts of the World: As Also for Collecting, Preserving, and Sending Natural Things. Being an Attempt to Settle an Universal Correspondence for the Advancement of Knowledge both Natural and Civil. Drawn up at the Request of a Person of Honour: and presented to the Royal Society,* with introduction by V. A. Eyles, Sherborn Fund Facsimilis (London: Society for the Bibliography of Natural History, 1973).

12. Information on the earliest known instructions, including some detail on the contents of these early publications, is found in Stresemann, *Ornithology,* 26, 47–48, 53, 79, 179, 294–95, 298.

13. Although the National Institute and the American Association for the Advancement of Science were better prepared to deal with the national collections than were local scientific societies, neither national organization had the institutional framework needed to cope with the large quantity of specimens deposited at the Patent Office before 1857 or at the Smithsonian after 1857. See A. Hunter Dupree, *Science in the Federal Government: A History of Policies and Activities to 1940* (Cambridge: Harvard University Press, Belknap Press, 1957); and Sally Gregory Kohlstedt, *The Formation of the American Scientific Community: The American Association for the Advancement of Science, 1848–1860* (Urbana: University of Illinois Press, 1976).

14. SIAR 1877, 105–11. See also Kellogg, "Century of Progress," 133; and Dall, *Baird,* 248–49.

15. P. L. Farber, *The Emergence of Ornithology as a Scientific Discipline, 1760–1850* (Boston: D. Reidel, 1982), cited in Mayr, *Growth of Biological Thought*, 170.

16. Albert Gunther, *A Century of Zoology at the British Museum: Through the Lives of Two Keepers, 1815–1914* (Kent, England: William Dawson and Sons, Cannon House, 1975), 111. See also chaps. 4–6 and 11.

17. The transformation of ethnology as a discipline within the humanities into anthropology as a social science has been identified with the mid-nineteenth century in a study of the Peabody Museum of American Archaeology and Ethnology; see C. M. Hinsley, Jr., "From Shell-Heaps to Stelae," in *Objects and Others: Essays on Museums and Material Culture*, ed. George W. Stocking, Jr. (Madison: University of Wisconsin Press, 1985), 51. See also Elman R. Service, *A Century of Controversy: Ethnological Issues from 1860 to 1960* (New York: Academic Press, 1985).

18. George Gibbs, "Instructions for Archaeological Investigations in the U. States," SIAR 1861, 392–96, and "Instructions for Research Relative to the Ethnology and Philology of America" [prepared 1863], Smithsonian Misc. Coll., vol. 7, no. 160 (1866), 2–47. Also important was Lewis H. Morgan, "Suggestions Relative to an Ethnological Map of North America," SIAR 1861, 297–98.

19. James Urry, "A History of Field Methods," in *Ethnographic Research: A Guide to General Conduct*, ed. R. F. Ellen (New York: Academic Press, 1984), 35–61, is an especially good source for information on the development of European fieldwork traditions. Urry devotes considerably less space to American developments, however, and he gives the Smithsonian initiatives relatively less space than they deserve.

20. J. Henry, introductory remarks to Gibbs, "Instructions for Research."

CHAPTER 3

1. Kennicott to Baird, 18 Dec. 1860, SIA, RU 7215, Box 13.

2. Lord Napier to Gov. George Simpson, 19 Mar. 1859, HBCA, PAM, D.5/48, fo. 403.

3. See E. E. Rich, *The History of the Hudson's Bay Company, 1670–1870*, vol. 1 (London: Hudson's Bay Record Society, 1959); Sir John Clapham, introduction to *Minutes of the Hudson's Bay Company, 1671–1674*, ed. E. E. Rich (Toronto: Champlain Society, 1942), xxvi–xxviii; R. P. Stearns, "The Royal Society and the Company," *The Beaver* (June 1945): 8–13.

4. "London Correspondence Book Outward," HBCA, PAM, A.6/5, fo. 96d.

5. Richard Glover, introduction to *Andrew Graham's Observations on Hudson Bay, 1767–1791*, ed. Glyndwr Williams, vol. 27 (London: Hudson's Bay Record Society, 1969), xiv–xv, xxiii. See also Stearns, "The Royal Society and the Company."

6. M. L. Tyrwhitt-Drake, "David Douglas," *DCB* 6:218–20.

7. See Grace Lee Nute, "A Botanist at Fort Colvile," *The Beaver* (Sept. 1946): 28–31; Suzanne Zeller, *Inventing Canada: Early Victorian Science and the Idea of*

a Transcontinental Nation (Toronto: University of Toronto Press, 1987), 212; and Thomas, "Smithsonian and HBC," 285.

8. McDonald, for example, corresponded with William Hooker, was an honorary member of the London Botanical Society, and was a contributor to the British Museum. Information on McDonald's scientific activities comes from Nute, "Botanist," 27, and from McDonald, *Peace River: A Canoe Voyage from Hudson's Bay to the Pacific, by the Late Sir George Simpson in 1828*, ed. Malcolm McLeod (Ottawa: J. Durie and Son, 1872). *Peace River* is a journal McDonald kept while part of Simpson's expedition to the Pacific in which he recorded his observations on the climate, soils, resources, and potential for agricultural settlement in the Northwest.

9. Stewart, "George Simpson," 4–9.

10. An enumeration and brief description of northern expeditions can be found in Alan Cooke and Clive Holland, *The Exploration of Northern Canada, 500 to 1920: A Chronology* (Toronto: Arctic Press, 1978).

11. Resolution 87, Minutes of Council, Northern Department, 1851. Resolution 88 directed Hudson's Bay Company officers to keep an account of the costs expended with regard to the British search expeditions and to forward that account to Lachine for settlement with the British government; HBCA, PAM, B.239/k/3, p. 21. See also "Correspondence regarding Arctic Medals and Certificates of Claim," HBCA, PAM, E.15/11.

12. Simpson to B. R. Ross, 15 June 1859, HBCA, PAM, B.200/b/34; Simpson to Henry, 28 Mar. 1859, SIA, HBC Corr. Coll., Folder 38; "Circular to Officers of the Hudson's Bay Company," Smithsonian Misc. Coll., vol. 2, no. 137 (1862), 7–8.

13. See "Subscriptions to Kennicott's Exploration of the Hudson's Bay Territories," Smithsonian Institution Exploration, 1852–76, HBC Territories Expeditions, 1859–62, SIA, RU 7002, Box 66. An account of Kennicott's expenditures is also available in "Smithsonian Institution, in Account with the Honble Hudson's Bay Comp," 1863–66, SIA, RU 7215, Folder 33.

14. On exploration in early nineteenth-century America, see, for example, William H. Goetzmann, *Exploration and Empire: The Explorer and the Scientist in the Winning of the American West* (New York: W. W. Norton, 1966) and *New Land, New Men: America and the Second Great Age of Discovery* (New York: Penguin Books, 1987).

15. For an extensive discussion of northern transportation and communication routes, see Kennicott to Baird, 27 July 1859, SIA, RU 7215, Box 13. For information on travel arrangements between Fort Garry and St. Paul, see letters from Clare to Baird, 1866, SIA, HBC Corr. Coll., Folder 8. For a description of Red River carts—two-wheeled wagons constructed entirely of wood and drawn by oxen or horses—see J. J. Hargrave, *Red River* (Montreal: John Lovell, 1874; reprint, Altona, Man.: Friesen Printers, 1977), 58–59.

16. Deignan, "HBC and Smithsonian," 3–7, made the same point many years ago, but his assessment of Kennicott's 1859 expedition was intuitive rather than based on a comparison of the two expeditions.

17. Biographical information on Robert Kennicott (1835–1866) and his father, John, has been obtained from James, introduction to *First Scientific Exploration*, 1–6, and from K. B. Sterling, introduction to *Bairdian Period*. Information on Robert Kennicott can also be found in Donald Zochert, "Notes on a Young Naturalist," *Audubon* (Mar. 1980): 34–47; G. L. Nute, "Kennicott in the North," *The Beaver* (Sept. 1943): 28–32; "Biography of Robert Kennicott," *Transactions of the Chicago Academy of Sciences* 1 (1867–69): 133–226; and *BDAS*, 145.

18. See Mary Kennicott's correspondence with Dall, SIA, RU 7073, Box 12; and John Kennicott to Baird, 17 Dec. 1857, SIA, RU 7002, Box 26.

19. On scientific training in North America in the early nineteenth century, see William Smallwood, *Natural History and the American Mind* (New York: Columbia University Press, 1941), 42–100, 285–336.

20. John Kennicott to Baird, 28 Nov. 1856, 6 June 1857, SIA, RU 7002, Box 26.

21. "Jared Potter Kirtland," *BDAS*, 147–48.

22. James, *First Scientific Exploration*, cites a letter written by Kirkland supporting the assertion that Kirkland was responsible for the development of Kennicott's career as a northern naturalist: Letter of Dr. Kirkland, 5 Apr. 1867, *Executive Documents*, 40th Cong., 2d sess., H. Doc. 177, 31. Information on Kennicott's studies with Kirtland is found in James, *First Scientific Exploration*, 111, although James incorrectly refers to Cook's book as *Vancouver*. Cook's book was one of the best-known English sourcebooks on Russian America; most eighteenth- and early nineteenth-century works containing information on the Northwest Coast were in Russian or German. See Wickersham, *Bibliography of Alaskan Literature*, and Dall, Appendix H, *Alaska and Its Resources*.

23. SIAR 1853, 56; 1854, 44; 1855, 46.

24. Dall, *Baird*, 333; Baird to R. Kennicott, 6 Oct. 1853, in Dall, *Baird*, 307–8; J. Kennicott to Baird, 17 Dec. 1857, SIA, RU 7002, Box 26.

25. SIAR 1855, 46.

26. Thomas, "Smithsonian and HBC," 290.

27. Donald Gunn to Baird, SIA, RU 52, Box 7, vol. 2, 329; Baird to Gunn, 11 Oct. 1855, 10 Apr. 1856, SIA, RU 57, Box 2.

28. Public lectures were given at the Smithsonian by E. K. Kane in 1852 and by John Rae in 1858 (SIAR 1852, 28; 1858, 43).

29. James, *First Scientific Exploration*, 6; manuscript excerpt from Lucy Baird's biography of her father, PAM, MG1 B18.

30. See the following publications by Kennicott: "Descriptions of New and Known North American Serpents," in *Report on the United States and Mexican Boundary Survey, Made under the Direction of the Secretary of the Interior, by William H. Emory, Major First Cavalry, and the United States Commissioner*, vol. 2, *Reptiles* (Washington, D.C.: C. Wendell, 1857–59), pp. 14–23 and pls. iii–viii, xii, xix, xxi; "Descriptions of New and Known North American Serpents," in *Pacific Railroad Survey Reports*, vol. 10, pp. 10–11 and pl. xi of Williamson Report, p. 19 and pl. xvii of Beckwith Report, pp. 39–43 of Whipple Report, and

NOTES TO PAGES 48-50

vol. 12, pt. 2, pp. 296–300 and pls. xiii–xvi, xix, xx, and xxii of Cooper Report. Kennicott had some early publications in the *Proceedings of the Academy of Natural Science of Philadelphia:* "Description of a New Snake from Illinois," vol. 8 (Apr. 1856), 95–96; "Notes on *Coluber calligaster* of Say, and Descriptions of New Species of Serpents in the Collection of the Northwestern University of Evanston," vol. 11 (Mar. 1859), 98–100. See also "Catalogue of Animals Observed in Cook County, Illinois," *Transactions of the Illinois State Agricultural Society* 1 [ca. 1855]: 577–95.

31. Kennicott's article was published in *Report of the Commissioner of Patents for the Years 1856–1858: Agriculture* (Washington, D.C., 1856–58), reprinted in Sterling, *Bairdian Period.* The scientific community's assessment of it is noted in James, *First Scientific Exploration,* 3.

32. Laurence Clarke, Jr. (1832–1890), the clerk in charge of Fort Rae, was born in Fermoy, Ireland, but went to Rupert's Land after having lived in the West Indian tropics. He joined the Hudson's Bay Company as a clerk in 1851 and was sent directly to the Mackenzie River District. He rose through the ranks fairly quickly, becoming a chief trader in 1867, a factor in 1872, and a chief factor in 1875. Clarke also became a prominent member of the community of Prince Albert, Saskatchewan, where he settled in 1878. See Stanley Gordon, "Lawrence [*sic*] Clarke," *DCB* 11:194–95, and HBCA, PAM, B.239/k/13.

33. Clarke to Baird, 21 June 1861, SIA, HBC Corr. Coll., Folder 9.

34. Kennicott's father was a physician but a "poor provider." By the 1850s he was in poor health, and when feeling well, he spent his time pursuing his horticultural interests. J. Kennicott to Baird, 28 Nov. 1856, SIA, RU 7002, Box 26.

35. Other scholars have commented on Kennicott's personal appeal to and influence over northerners, for example, J. A. James, G. L. Nute, and G. Thomas. A tabular presentation of the numbers of specimens donated to the Smithsonian appears in the Appendix. Note that the specimens that would normally have arrived in Washington in 1862 arrived late (SIAR 1863, 53).

36. R. Kennicott to Baird, 7 May 1859, SIA, RU 7002, Box 27. Kennicott's nickname is referred to in Hargrave, *Red River,* 246.

37. Jennifer S. H. Brown and Sylvia Van Kirk, "George Barnston," *DCB* 11:52–53; George A. Dunlop and C. P. Wilson, "George Barnston," *The Beaver* (Dec. 1941): 16–17.

38. Barnston to Baird, 23 June 1859, SIA, HBC Corr. Coll., Folder 2.

39. Information on the responsibilities of the overseas governor, and on Simpson himself, can be found in the following sources: H. A. Innis, introduction to *Minutes of Council, Northern Department of Rupert's Land, 1821–1831,* ed. R. Harvey Fleming, ser. ed. E. E. Rich (Toronto: Champlain Society, 1940), xiii; G. Williams, ed., *Hudson's Bay Miscellany, 1670–1870* (Winnipeg: Hudson's Bay Record Society, 1975), 153–66; John S. Galbraith, *The Little Emperor: Governor Simpson of the Hudson's Bay Company* (Toronto: Macmillan of Canada, 1976); Stewart, "George Simpson," 4–9.

40. Resolutions 76 and 77, Minutes of Council, Northern Department, 1859–60, HBCA, PAM, B.239/k/13.

41. Most of this information comes from Kennicott to Baird, 15 June 1859, SIA, RU 7215, Box 13, with the exception of the information on the special arrangements between Kennicott and B. R. Ross for sending written material, such as scientific articles, north. That information is referred to in a list of articles appended to Kennicott to Baird, 18 June 1859, SIA, RU 7215, Box 13.

42. Kennicott to Baird, 17 Nov. 1859, SIA, RU 7215, Box 13.

43. Kennicott was traveling with Charles Hubbard of Milwaukee. Hubbard had been brought up by Increase Lapham, who wrote *Antiquities of Wisconsin* (1846) and was a scientist and geologist for the state of Wisconsin (1873-75). Hubbard and Kennicott parted company at Fort Alexander, when Hubbard returned to the United States. For biographical information on Hubbard, see Kennicott to Baird, 18 Apr. 1859, SIA, RU 7215, Box 13. See also Kennicott to Baird, 16, 18 May 1859, SIA, RU 7215, Box 13, and SIAR 1859, 66.

44. Simpson's position—stated in Kennicott to Baird, 15 June 1859, SIA, RU 7215, Box 13—reflected Resolution 70, Standing Rules and Regulations of the Honorable Hudson's Bay Company, Minutes of Council, Northern Department, in which the council stipulated that missionaries and "strangers" traveling on company boats be charged 5d, with the costs of shipping freight and baggage priced according to the established tariff. See Minutes of Council, 1843-66, HBCA, PAM, B.239/k/24.

45. Brother Tadger was the nickname given William Kirkby, a clergyman with the Church Missionary Society who traveled to the north in the same boats as Kennicott. See Thomas C. B. Boon, "William West Kirkby, First Anglican Missionary to the Loucheux," *The Beaver* (Spring 1965): 36-43. The quotation is from Kennicott to Baird, 17 Nov. 1859, SIA, RU 7215, Box 13.

46. Debra Lindsay, "The Hudson's Bay Company–Smithsonian Connection and Fur Trade Intellectual Life: Bernard Rogan Ross, a Case Study," in *Le Castor Fait Tout,* Selected Papers of the Fifth North American Fur Trade Conference, 1985, ed. Bruce Trigger, Toby Morantz, and Louise Dechêne (Montreal: Lake St. Louis Historical Society, 1987), 587-617.

47. Kennicott wrote to Baird (8 July 1861, SIA, RU 7215, Box 13) that Ross had sung to him for two solid hours one evening and that the episode had been very taxing on their relationship. Ross also recorded local gossip in the *Athabasca and English River Inquirer;* see B. R. Ross, "Fur Trade Gossip Sheet," *The Beaver* (Spring 1955): 52. Examples of his poetry can be found in the McGowan Collection, HBCA, PAM, E.61/2, fos. 11-12, and in the Donald Ross Collection, PAM, MG1 D20 M310.

48. Ross mentions his acquaintance with Gibbs in a letter to Joseph Henry, 28 Nov. 1858, SIA, HBC Corr. Coll., Folder 36.

49. John Austin Stevens, Jr., "A Memorial of George Gibbs," SIAR 1873, 219-25.

50. Kennicott to Baird, 27 July 1859, SIA, RU 7215, Box 13.

51. Resolution 76, 1859-60; Resolution 78, 1860-61; and Resolution 84, 1861-62, Minutes of Council, Northern Department, HBCA, PAM, B.239/k/13.

52. Smithsonian responsibilities for freight are noted in "Smithsonian Institution, in Account with the Honble Hudson's Bay Comp," 1863-66. Ross's new

arrangement is discussed in Kennicott to Baird, 17 Nov. 1859, SIA, RU 7215, Box 13.

53. Clarke to Kennicott, 16 Jan. 1865, SIA, HBC Corr. Coll., Box 1.

54. See Minutes of Council, Northern Department, 1843–66 and 1865, HBCA, PAM, B.239/k/24 and B.239/k/3, p. 302.

55. Kennicott to Baird, 29 June 1860, SIA, RU 7215, Box 13.

56. In this quotation Kennicott's reference to "Reed" is obfuscated by misspelling. Kennicott is referring to John Reid (ca. 1826–1895), who resided in Eday Parish, Scotland, before joining the Hudson's Bay Company as a laborer. He served as midman, steersman, fisherman, and interpreter before being promoted to postmaster in 1857. According to Kennicott's description, he was "a postmaster raised from a common man and uneducated but very conceited—tho obliging and not a bad fellow at all" (Kennicott to Baird, 29 June 1860, SIA, RU 7215, Box 13). Reid was postmaster in charge for 12 of the 15 years that he spent at Big Island, but he was not given a clerkship until 1877. In 1885 he was promoted to junior chief trader, the highest position that he obtained during his career with the HBC. For information on Reid, see HBCA biographical files. For details of his postings, see Minutes of Council, Northern Department, HBCA, PAM, B.239/g/83 and 88–100; B.239/k/3, pp. 163, 183, 202; D.38/26, fos. 8, 12, 14, 18, 22d, 23, 24, 28.

The quotation in the text comes from Kennicott to Baird, 29 June 1860, SIA, RU 7215, Box 13. For evidence of Ross's appropriations, see Reid to Baird, 8 Dec. 1863, 6 Dec. 1864, SIA, HBC Corr. Coll., Folder 35; Kennicott to Baird, 1 Sept. 1860, 23 July 1861, 21 Jan. 1862, SIA, RU 7215, Box 13; MacFarlane to Baird, 16 May 1861, SIA, RU 7215, Box 14.

57. Kennicott to Baird, 29 June 1860, SIA, RU 7215, Box 13.

58. See Appendix.

59. Julian Onion (1839–1907) made his way to Fort Simpson following a posting with the Royal Canadian Rifles at Red River. The young officer had been born in Ceylon but was of English descent, and his career in the army was assured by his training at Woolwich. Army life was apparently less lucrative than the £75 that he was offered for a clerkship with the HBC; Onion joined the company immediately after selling his lieutenant's commission and obtaining a release from the rifle corps. Onion's northern career with the HBC lasted 43 years, and he became a chief factor in 1884, although he assumed his commission under the name Camsell. (In 1876 Onion had traveled to London to change his surname from that of his father's family to that of his mother's.) See Charles Camsell, *Son of the North* (Toronto: Ryerson Press, 1954), 2–4. Information on Onion's salary and postings with the company can be found in Resolution 74, Minutes of Council, Northern Department, 1862, HBCA, PAM, B.239/k/13; Alexander Morris Papers, PAM, MG12 B1 #1934; and J. L. Gaudet, "Chief Trader Charles Philip Gaudet," *The Beaver* (Sept. 1935): 45. For details of Kennicott's journey north, see Kennicott to Baird, 18 June 1859, SIA, RU 7215, Box 13.

60. For a description of clerks' duties at HBC posts, see Isaac Cowie, *The Company of Adventurers* (Toronto: William Briggs, 1913), 225–31.

61. Swanston was the postmaster at Fort Simpson when Kennicott arrived in 1859, but he was soon promoted to apprentice clerk, with Andrew Flett replacing him as postmaster. Swanston was promoted to clerk in 1869. Flett was from the parish of Orphir, Scotland, when he joined the company in 1846 as a laborer. He retired after 36 years of active service, having risen to the rank of clerk in 1868. For information on the career progression of Swanston and Flett, see Resolution 13, 1858; Resolution 12, 1859; and Resolution 12, 1860, Minutes of Council, Northern Department, HBCA, PAM, B.239/k/13. See also HBCA, PAM, B.239/g/86–99; B.239/k/3, pp. 202, 221, 242, 264, 286, 309, 330, 351, 375, 406, 431; B.239/k/4, fos. 1d, 10d, 20, 30d, 48, 54d; B.239/u/1, fo. 122; B.239/u/4, no. 87.

62. Cowie, *Company of Adventurers*, 272–78.

63. Little is known about Alexander Mackenzie, the man who sent some of the first HBC collections south. Serving as a clerk in various posts throughout the district until he retired in 1868, he was one of the first HBC men to embrace collecting, but his contributions were small and sporadic. Collections were received in his name on only two occasions, and they accounted for only slightly more than 1 percent of the total number from the district between 1860 and 1869. See Resolution 74, Minutes of Council, Northern Department, 1859 and 1870, HBCA, PAM, B.239/k/13.

James Dunlop, from the parish of Wandsworth, Scotland, joined the company as an apprentice clerk in 1856, serving his apprenticeship in the Mackenzie River District. He was promoted to the rank of clerk for the 1861–62 outfit and retained that position until he retired from the service in 1867. See HBCA biographical files and HBCA, PAM, B.56/a/14; B.56/d/11-13; B.239/g/107; B.239/k/3, pp. 142, 163, 182, 202, 223, 241, 263, 285, 307, 328.

Nicol Taylor (b. ca. 1817) signed on with the company in 1835 and served as midman, laborer, and fisherman until 1849, when he was promoted to interpreter. In 1855 he was promoted to postmaster, and in 1863 he was finally made clerk in charge of Fort Norman. He served as a clerk in the Mackenzie River District until 1879. See HBCA biographical files and HBCA, PAM, B.235/k/1, fos. 20d, 48d; B.239/g/75–96; B.239/k/1, fos. 1d, 10d, 20; B.239/k/3, pp. 264, 286, 308, 330, 351, 375, 405, 431.

James Flett (ca. 1825–1899) also signed on with the HBC in Scotland. Joining the company as a laborer in 1845, he was a laborer, fisherman, bowman, guide, and interpreter until 1861, when he was promoted to postmaster in charge of La Pierre's House. He served as postmaster in the Mackenzie River District until 1875, when he was made a clerk, a position he retained until his retirement in 1891. See HBCA biographical files and HBCA, PAM, A.32/28, fos. 243, 245, 253; B.114/d/2, fo. 7d; B.235/g/1–11; B.235/k/1, fos. 1d, 20, 30d, 48d, 54d, 80, 91, 100d; B.235/u/5; B.239/g/85–113; B.239/k/3, pp. 221, 243, 264, 287, 309, 330, 351, 375, 376, 405, 406, 431, 432; B.239/u/1–5; D.38/4, pp. 42–43, 58–59, 70–71; D.38/5; D.38/6b, fo. 64; D.38/49; D.38/66, fo. 64.

64. William Lucas Hardisty (ca. 1822–1881), the son of Chief Trader Richard Hardisty and an Algonkian woman, was in charge at Resolution when Kennicott visited the fort. The younger Hardisty began his HBC career in the Mackenzie

River District in 1842, and as was often the case with second-generation fur trade families, he entered the service with a noncommissioned posting. He advanced through the ranks with relative rapidity, especially in view of the HBC's discriminatory policy toward employees of native ancestry. In 1851 he went to Fort Yukon as a clerk, and by 1858 he had been promoted to chief trader. Following his promotion he was stationed at Fort Resolution one season before he moved on to Fort Liard, where he remained until 1862. He then left that minor post for Fort Simpson, where he assumed responsibility for the Mackenzie River District until his retirement in 1878. See J. S. H. Brown, "William Lucas Hardisty," *DCB* 11:384-85; Carol M. Judd, "Employment Opportunities for Mixed Bloods in the Hudson's Bay Company to 1870," HBCA, PAM, 1979-21.

65. Hardisty to Baird, 24 Nov. 1867, SIA, HBC Corr. Coll., Folder 22.

66. Clarke's poor showing at the Smithsonian might also be explained by his departure from the Mackenzie River District in 1863. He was posted to Fort à la Corne, in the Saskatchewan District, where he was preoccupied with encroachments from rival traders. In addition, the Saskatchewan Indians would seldom collect natural history specimens. They were, Clarke wrote, either at war among themselves or suffering the consequences of measles and influenza epidemics. See Clarke to Baird, 21 Jan. 1866, 1 Oct. 1867, SIA, HBC Corr. Coll., Folder 9.

67. Kennicott to Baird, 18 Dec. 1860, SIA, RU 7215, Box 13.

68. Lockhart had been a resident of Lachine, the HBC's overseas headquarters, when he joined the service in 1849. He was only 22 years old when he received his first posting as an apprentice clerk (Simpson to James Hargrave, 28 June 1849, HBCA, PAM, B.239/c/5). In 1854 he was promoted to clerk and was dispatched to one of the exploratory and search expeditions to the Arctic (HBCA, PAM, E.15/11). He was transferred to the Mackenzie River District the next year, was placed in charge of Fort Yukon in 1860, and one year later was promoted to chief trader (Minutes of Council, Northern Department, 1861, HBCA, PAM, B.239/k/13). For Lockhart's views on northern life, see Lockhart to Baird, 5 Feb. 1867, SIA, HBC Corr. Coll., Folder 26.

69. Lockhart to Baird, 21, 28 Nov. 1864, SIA, HBC Corr. Coll. Folder 26; Kennicott to Baird, 25 Oct. 1862, 18 Oct. 1863, SIA, RU 7215, Box 13.

70. Kennicott to Lucy Baird, 18 Dec. 1860, SIA, RU 7002, Box 37.

71. William Brass, originally from the parish of Sandwich in the Orkney Islands, joined the HBC in 1845 as a laborer. Promoted to the rank of postmaster in 1859, he served under Lockhart and Jones for two years before moving on to forts Halkett, Nelson, and Hay River. In 1860 he was promoted to clerk in charge, and he became a free agent in 1887. In 1883 Brass moved to Manitoba, intending to retire, but he returned north within the year, after finding himself unable to adjust to life in the south. See HBCA biographical files and HBCA, PAM, B.200/f/1, fos. 4d, 5; B.200/f/2, fos. 2, 8, 12, 14, 19; B.239/g/85-98, 112, 113; B.239/k/3, 183, 202, 221, 242, 264, 286, 308; D.24/3, p. 57; D.24/5, fo. 30.

Strachan Jones was the son of Thomas Mercer Jones, onetime chief officer of the Canada Company in the colonies, and Elizabeth Mary Strachan, daughter of Anglican bishop John Strachan. See Roger D. Hall, "Thomas Mercer Jones,"

DCB 9:415–17; S. Jones to S. F. Baird, 9 Apr. 1867, SIA, HBC Corr. Coll., Folder 24.

72. Kennicott to Baird, 23 June 1861, SIA, RU 7215, Box 13.

73. Charles Gaudet (1827–1917) was born and raised in Montreal, joining the HBC in 1852. Initially posted to Fort Resolution, he was sent in 1854 to Fort Yukon, where he stayed two years before being posted to Fort McPherson, or the "Peel's River" Post. Gaudet remained at Peel's River until the 1863–64 outfit, when he was reassigned to Fort Good Hope. He was reportedly fluent in "Eskimo" and would have had many opportunities to use such a skill at Good Hope, where he stayed until 1866. In fact Gaudet sent out at least 35 "Eskimo" artifacts in 1866 (Registers, Accession Records, Department of Anthropology, NMNH, vols. 1–3, SIA, RU 6690T). He became a clerk in 1863 and was eventually promoted to chief trader, staying with the company until 1911. See HBCA Search File: "Misc. G Folder People"; Gaudet, "Chief Trader Gaudet"; J. L. Gaudet to MacFarlane, 3 Apr. 1918, Edward Alexander Preble Papers, 1887–1957, SIA, RU 7252, Box 3, Folder 13. (MacFarlane forwarded Gaudet's letter to Preble, who was compiling biographical data on the HBC collectors at the Smithsonian.) There is some discrepancy between the above sources and the HBC Minutes of Council, Northern Department, regarding the year Charles Gaudet joined the company. In the minutes, he is registered as a postmaster in 1851, at £25, the lowest rate of pay (Resolution 68, HBCA, PAM, B.239/k/12, p. 322). See also Kennicott's description of life at Gaudet's post in "A Rubbaboo Journal for Friends at Home," in *First Scientific Exploration,* ed. James, 85–135.

74. Kennicott to L. Baird, 18 Dec. 1860, SIA, RU 7002, Box 37.

75. Kennicott to S. F. Baird, 29 Oct. 1862, SIA, RU 7215, Box 13. See also the pamphlet "A Brief Sketch of the Life and Services of Retired Chief Factor R. MacFarlane, 1852–1913," by R. R. MacFarlane (PAM, MG14 C23, Box 2, #47), extracted from Frank Howard Schofield, *The Story of Manitoba,* vol. 3 (Winnipeg: S. J. Clarke, 1913). The pamphlet differs from the biography found in Schofield's volume; the former is significantly longer and contains several highly subjective comments on the part of its author—MacFarlane himself.

76. Gov. William Mactavish to Baird, 29 Jan. 1866, SIA, HBC Corr. Coll., Folder 33.

77. MacFarlane, "Retired Chief Factor," 5.

78. Ibid.

79. Hardisty to Kennicott, 30 Nov. 1864, SIA, HBC Corr. Coll., Folder 22.

80. MacFarlane, "Retired Chief Factor," 3, and "Notes on and List of Birds and Eggs Collected in Arctic America, 1861–1866," *Proceedings of the United States National Museum* 14 (1891): 415. James Lockhart also refers to the scarlet fever and measles epidemics of 1865 in a letter to Baird, 18 Dec. 1865, SIA, HBC Corr. Coll., Folder 26.

CHAPTER 4

1. Few scholarly studies have been made of northern North American ethnoscience, especially with regard to native classifications of animal life. Julia

Cruikshank has done some preliminary work in "Legend and Landscape: Convergence of Oral and Scientific Traditions with Special Reference to the Yukon Territory, Canada" (thesis, Diploma in Polar Studies, Scott Polar Research Institute, Cambridge, England, 1980), but Keith Thomas, *Man and the Natural World: Changing Attitudes in England, 1500–1800* (London: Penguin Books, 1983), provides a broader conceptual framework for understanding the differences between "learned" and "folk" natural history, or what might also be called scientific and pre-scientific worldviews. Thomas states that the popular conception and early application of the study of nature in England were determined by practical considerations such as edibility or domesticity. He contends that this anthropocentric conception of natural history was then replaced by a learned variety of natural history, whereupon nature came to be studied in its own right, albeit as evidence of God's existence and divine purpose. The modern, or learned, conception of natural history, which attempted to give order to the plants, animals, and minerals found on earth—through the collection, enumeration, description, and classification of each and every specimen—superseded the popular, or folk, approach to the study of nature. Nature was soon identified, categorized, and classified according to morphological criteria. Less than 50 years later a standardized Latin nomenclature had virtually eradicated popular classifications by educated persons.

2. Newton, "Suggestions for Forming Collections," 10–22.

3. T. M. Brewer, "Instructions for Oological Collecting," Smithsonian Misc. Coll., vol. 2 (1862), 3. (This volume of Smithsonian Misc. Coll. also includes reprints of "Instructions in Reference to Collecting Nests and Eggs of North American Birds" [Jan. 1860] and "Circular in Reference to Collecting Nests and Eggs of North American Birds" [Feb. 1861].)

4. Douglas Cole, *Captured Heritage: The Scramble for Northwest Coast Artifacts* (Vancouver: Douglas and McIntyre, 1985), has demonstrated the economic value of ethnological artifacts in his study of collecting on the Northwest Coast. He concludes: "The collecting process was a trading relationship affected by normal economic factors of supply and demand, competition, accessibility, costs of transportation, by wars and trade cycles, by ethnological fashion and museum budgets" (p. 310).

5. Kennicott to Baird, 29 June 1860, SIA, RU 7215, Box 13.

6. Information on the goods traded for specimens comes from a list of trade goods, personal provisions, and scientific materials and apparatus requested by Kennicott, April and June 1860, in Smithsonian Institution Exploration, 1852–76, HBC Territories Expeditions, 1859–62, SIA, RU 7002, Box 66; and Kennicott to Baird, 29 June, 1 Sept. 1860, SIA, RU 7215, Box 13.

7. Kennicott to Baird, 18 Dec. 1860, SIA, RU 7215, Box 13.

8. Smithsonian Institution Exploration, SIA, RU 7002, Box 66.

9. Marriages between Europeans and Athapaskans and between Europeans and "mixed-bloods" were still common in the Mackenzie River District at midcentury among members of the servant class, and both James Sibbeston and Reid had "pure Indian" wives. Gaudet had a "mixed-blood" wife and family, as did

Andrew Flett and all the laborers. Jane, the wife of James Dunlop, was of mixed ancestry, and James Flett had married a native woman. References regarding the fur traders' marital relations are dispersed throughout Kennicott's correspondence. "List of Presents Sent to Arctic Correspondents," SIA, HBC Corr. Coll., Folder 41, identifies fur trade wives according to ancestry. See also Kennicott to Baird, 21 Jan. 1862, SIA, RU 7215, Box 13; Lockhart to Kennicott, 21 Nov. 1864, SIA, HBC Corr. Coll., Folder 26.

10. "Distribution of Presents to the Wives of Correspondents of S.I. in the Mackenzies River District, Spring of 1867," SIA, RU 7002, Box 66.

11. Brewer, "Instructions for Oological Collecting," 3, 13.

12. Numerous references may be found on the methods of identification used by northern collectors. The best account is in Kennicott to Baird, 21 Jan. 1862, SIA, RU 7215, Box 13, but see also the following: Kennicott to Baird, 17 Nov. 1859, SIA, RU 7215, Box 13; and Ross to Baird, 15 Apr. 1861; Barnston to Baird, 28 Jan. 1862; Gunn to Baird, 3 Jan. 1866, SIA, HBC Corr. Coll., Folders 20, 36.

13. Kennicott to Baird, 21 Jan. 1862, SIA, RU 7215, Box 13.

14. Ross to Baird, 20 June 1860, 15 Apr., 20 Nov. 1861; Barnston to Baird, 28 Jan. 1862, SIA, HBC Corr. Coll., Folders 2, 36, 37.

15. Ross to Baird, 20 June 1860, SIA, HBC Corr. Coll., Folder 36.

16. Gaudet to Kennicott, 14 Sept. 1864; Jones to Baird, 27 Nov. 1865; Lockhart to Baird, 28 Nov. 1864; Lockhart to Kennicott, 5 Dec. 1864, SIA, HBC Corr. Coll., Folders 18, 24, 26.

17. Kennicott to Baird, 23 June 1861, SIA, RU 7215, Box 13.

18. Barnston supervised, for example, the skinning, disjointing, boiling, and scraping of bones done by a "halfbreed" hunter, a young native man, and two women. See Barnston to Baird, 15 Mar. 1860, SIA, HBC Corr. Coll., Folder 2.

19. Barnston to Baird, 28 Jan. 1862, SIA, HBC Corr. Coll., Folder 2.

20. Ibid. See also Barnston's "Remarks on the Genus *Lutra,* and on the Species Inhabiting North America," *Canadian Naturalist and Geologist* 8 (1863): 147–59; and E. Raymond Hall and Keith R. Kelson, *The Mammals of North America,* vol. 2 (New York: Ronald Press, 1959), 944–45.

21. See Gunn to Baird, 4 June 1856, 24 Dec. 1858, SIA, RU 305, Reels 6, 7; 2 June 1857, SIA, RU 7215, Box 10; May 1862, 3 Aug. 1864, SIA, HBC Corr. Coll., Folder 20.

22. Gunn to Baird, 16 June 1866, SIA, HBC Corr. Coll., Folder 20.

23. These were the projected costs given Baird for native assistants when Gunn was seeking financial support for his trip to Lake Winnipeg. Gunn to Baird, 27 Dec. 1864, SIA, HBC Corr. Coll., Folder 20.

24. This information was found in a list of specimens sent by J. Isbister to Donald Gunn, n.d., Donald Gunn Collection, SIA, RU 7215, Box 10, and in Gunn to Baird, 4 June 1856, 24 Dec. 1858, SIA, RU 305, Reels 6, 7.

25. Such comments appear throughout the correspondence between the HBC collectors and the Smithsonian. Examples can be found in any of the letters contained in HBC Corr. Coll., but see specifically Isbister to Gunn, n.d., SIA, RU 7215, Box 10, and the following from SIA, HBC Corr. Coll., Folders 9, 32, 36:

Ross to Baird, 10 Nov. 1860; Clarke to Baird, 21 June 1861; W. J. McLean to Kennicott, 17 Nov. 1864; McLean to Baird, 17 Nov. 1867.

26. The contributions made by native assistants in MacFarlane's collection are even referred to in Baird, Brewer, and Ridgway, *History of North American Birds*, 2:205, 394; 3:309, 460. For MacFarlane's comments on native collectors, see MacFarlane to Baird, 6 May 1863, SIA, RU 7215, Box 14.

27. F. Whymper, *Travel and Adventure in the Territory of Alaska, Formerly Russian America—Now Ceded to the United States, and in Various Other Parts of the North Pacific* (New York: Harper and Bros., 1869), 345–50. See also "Comparative Vocabulary of Animal and Bird Names," no. 163, Slave and Kutchin, Department of Anthropology, NMNH, Smithsonian Institution.

28. Kennicott to Baird, 29 June 1860, SIA, RU 7215, Box 13.

29. Ibid., 17 Nov. 1859.

30. Ibid., 23 Mar. 1860.

31. Ibid., 21 Jan. 1862.

32. Ross to Baird, 20 June 1860, SIA, HBC Corr. Coll., Folder 36.

33. SIA, RU 7215, Box 29, Folder: B. R. Ross.

34. Kennicott to Baird, 29 June 1860, SIA, RU 7215, Box 13.

35. Ibid.

36. Ibid., 21 Jan. 1862.

37. Ibid., 17 Nov. 1859, 18 Dec. 1860.

38. Ibid., 18 Dec. 1860.

39. "Journal of Robert Kennicott," 83.

40. Ibid., 84.

41. Kennicott to Baird, 23 June 1861, SIA, RU 7215, Box 13.

42. Jones to Baird, 8 July 1867, SIA, HBC Corr. Coll., Folder 24.

43. SIAR 1868, 22. See also MacFarlane, "Retired Chief Factor," 3.

44. MacFarlane to Kennicott, 7 Feb. 1865, SIA, RU 7215, Box 14.

45. Lockhart to Baird, 24 June 1861, SIA, HBC Corr. Coll., Folder 23.

46. Kennicott to Baird, 23 June 1861, SIA, RU 7215, Box 13. Kennicott planned to have Hoole, who spoke Kutchin "*better* than a native," assist in a study of the Kutchin language. Even though Hoole's interpretive activities were his most important function, Kennicott also expected him to prepare the oological specimens personally. The Grove was the name given the Kennicott family home in Illinois.

47. Ibid.

48. Ibid., 29 Oct. 1862.

49. MacFarlane to Baird, 28 July 1862, SIA, RU 7215, Box 14.

50. Ibid., 13 July 1863.

51. Ibid., 6 May 1863.

52. For example, MacFarlane took another party of native collectors on a second overland expedition in search of eggs, doubling the number of native assistants he had taken on his journey to the Arctic Ocean in the spring of 1864. See MacFarlane to Baird, 28 July 1862, 10 May 1864, 20 Jan. 1866, SIA, RU 7215, Box 14, and a letter written during 1863, SIA, HBC Corr. Coll., Folder 30. Other

correspondence between MacFarlane and Baird also mentions MacFarlane's reliance on native collectors; see letters dated 3 Sept. 1862 and 9 Feb. 1863, SIA, RU 7215, Box 14.

CHAPTER 5

1. Information on early nineteenth-century European anthropological collections can be found in William Ryan Chapman, "Arranging Ethnology: A.H.L.F. Pitt Rivers and the Typological Tradition," in *Objects and Others,* ed. Stocking, 23–24; and Erna V. Siebert, "Northern Athapaskan Collections of the First Half of the Nineteenth Century," *Arctic Anthropology* 17-1 (1980): 49–60. See also Edward P. Alexander, *Museums in Motion: An Introduction to the History and Functions of Museums* (Nashville: American Association for State and Local History, 1987).

Harvard University accepted an endowment to build a museum dedicated to archaeological and ethnological collections in 1866. The Peabody Museum of American Archaeology and Ethnology emerged at the same time that Smithsonian scientists were adding anthropology to their roster of activities. See Hinsley, "From Shell-Heaps to Stelae," 49–74.

2. See Hinsley, "From Shell-Heaps to Stelae," 49–74; and John C. Ewers, "A Century of American Indian Exhibits in the Smithsonian Institution," SIAR 1958, 514–15.

3. Andrew Murray (1812–1878) was a Scottish naturalist and collector often referred to in Ross's correspondence. He was a fellow of the Royal Society, Edinburgh; president of the Edinburgh Botanical Society (1858); secretary of the Royal Horticultural Society (1860); and a collector for the Industrial Museum of Scotland (Royal Scottish Museum). See *The Dictionary of National Biography: The Concise Dictionary,* pt. 1, *From the Beginnings to 1900* (Oxford: Oxford University Press, 1961), 920; and Robert Kerr, "For the Royal Scottish Museum," *The Beaver* (June 1953): 32–35. For the quotation cited, see Kennicott to Baird, 17 Nov. 1859, SIA, RU 7215, Box 13. For information on Ross's European scientific connections, see Bernard Rogan Ross Notebook, SIA, RU 7221.

4. On Gibbs's relationship with the Smithsonian, see Hinsley, *Savages and Scientists,* 51–56.

5. Ewers, "American Indian Exhibits," 514–15.

6. SIAR 1861, 394.

7. For a discussion of the psychological basis of the accumulative impulse underlying museum accessioning, see James Clifford, "Objects and Selves—An Afterword," in *Objects and Others,* ed. Stocking, 236–46. Clifford contends that museum collections reveal more about the cultural values of the collectors than they reveal about the cultures subjected to study. Stocking's examination of nineteenth-century anthropology supports Clifford's theory. Victorian society was fascinated with primitive technology because it illustrated the superiority of nineteenth-century Western technology. See also G. W. Stocking, Jr., prologue to

Victorian Anthropology (New York: Free Press, 1987), as well as Hinsley, *Savages and Scientists,* 41, and Glyn Daniels, "One Hundred Years of Old World Prehistory," in *One Hundred Years of Anthropology,* ed. J. O. Brew (Cambridge: Harvard University Press, 1968), 58.

8. Hinsley, *Savages and Scientists,* 41, 51–54, states that Gibbs's instructions were indicative of the interest in collecting Indian antiquities that was stimulated by Adolphe Morlot's article "General Views on Archaeology," SIAR 1860, 284–343.

9. Gibbs, "Instructions for Archaeological Investigation," 394.

10. Ibid.

11. Hinsley, *Savages and Scientists,* 21–22, 51–52, discusses the salvage ethos as personified by Gibbs. See also Gibbs, "Instructions for Research," 7. Hinsley states that Henry made a determined effort to disassociate the Smithsonian from physical anthropology (pp. 27–28), though Henry's efforts did not immediately reduce the demand for native craniums. By the 1860s skulls were viewed as a physiological corollary of the cultural differences associated with the historical development of primitive man, but polygenistic endeavors to prove multiple creations through comparative craniology had been largely replaced by attempts to correlate primitive cultural attributes with physiological evidence.

12. SIAR 1863, 53.

13. Registers, Accession Records, Department of Anthropology, NMNH, vols. 1–3, SIA, RU 6990T, and Computer Printout, Ident. MNH4 122G113, MNH-ANN.

14. Most of the models were purchased for less than £1 apiece, although articles of clothing could cost several pounds. Ordinary Indian clothing cost approximately £1, whereas a Kutchin chief's dress was purchased for several pounds. Kennicott to Baird, 17 Nov. 1859, SIA, RU 7215, Box 13; Ross to Baird, 10 Nov. 1860, SIA, HBC Corr. Coll., Folder 36.

15. Registers, Accession Records, Department of Anthropology, NMNH, vols. 1–3, SIA, RU 6990T, and Computer Printout, Ident. MNH4 122G113, MNH-ANN.

16. Hinsley, *Savages and Scientists,* 68, 91–93.

17. Gibbs, "Instructions for Research," 7.

18. The excerpt is from a manuscript draft (SIA, RU 7221) of Ross's published article on the Dene. This section was cut from the version that appears in SIAR 1866.

19. Gibbs to Henry, 18 Nov. 1862, SIAR 1862, 89–91. See also Lindsay, "HBC-Smithsonian Connection," 595.

20. Hinsley, *Savages and Scientists,* 8.

21. SIAR 1866, 301–27.

22. The quotations that follow are, in order, from Ross's essay "The Eastern Tinneh," SIAR 1868, 304, 305, 306, 307, 308, 310.

23. Gibbs, "Instructions for Research," 10.

24. Strachan Jones, "The Kutchin (Indian) Tribes," SIAR 1866, 325.

25. Mary Louise Pratt, "Fieldwork in Common Places," in *Writing Culture: The Poetics and Politics of Ethnography,* ed. James Clifford and George E.

Marcus (Berkeley and Los Angeles: University of California Press, 1986), 27–50; Vincent Crapanzano, "Hermes' Dilemma: The Masking of Subversion in Ethnographic Description," in *Writing Culture,* ed. Clifford and Marcus, 53.

26. See Robert F. Berkhofer, Jr., *The White Man's Indian: Images of the American Indian from Columbus to the Present* (New York: Alfred A. Knopf, 1978), and Stocking, *Victorian Anthropology.*

27. The relationship between fieldworkers and communities under study has not been well documented, but anthropologists acknowledge its importance to the success of field studies. See especially Elenore S. Bowen [Laura Bohannan], *Return to Laughter* (New York: Doubleday, 1964), and Napoleon Chagnon, *The Yanomamo: The Fierce People* (Toronto: Holt, Rinehart, and Winston, 1968). For a more analytical approach, see Pertti J. Pelto, *Anthropological Research: The Structure of Inquiry* (New York: Harper and Row, 1970). For a historical analysis of the relationships among anthropologists, material culture, and native populations, see D. Cole, "Tricks of the Trade: Northwest Coast Artifact Collecting, 1875–1925," *Canadian Historical Review* 63 (1982): 439–60; and Cole, *Captured Heritage,* 294–331.

28. Information on the contents of early exploration guides can be found in John Honigmann, *The Development of Anthropological Ideas* (Homewood, Ill.: Dorsey Press, 1976), 76n33, which specifically cites pp. 363–81 of Howard F. Cline, "The Relaciones Geograficas of the Spanish Indies, 1577–1586," *Hispanic American Historical Review* 44 (1964): 341–374.

29. SIAR 1860, republished in Smithsonian Misc. Coll., vol. 2 (1862).

30. MacFarlane to Baird, 6 May 1863, SIA, RU 7215, Box 14. See also L. H. Morgan, *Systems of Consanguinity and Affinity of the Human Family,* Smithsonian Contr. Knowl., vol. 17, no. 218 (1871) [originally accepted for publication in 1868; see SIAR 1868, 450], and *Ancient Society: Researches in the Lines of Human Progress from Savagery through Barbarism to Civilization* (New York: H. Holt, 1877).

31. Hardisty to Kennicott, 30 Nov. 1864, SIA, HBC Corr. Coll., Folder 22. Hardisty's contributions to Morgan's work can be found in Morgan, *Systems of Consanguinity and Affinity of the Human Family* (1871; reprint, Oosterhout, N.B., Netherlands, 1970), 291–382, as can Morgan's acknowledgment, 289.

32. Pelto, *Anthropological Research.* For a slightly different application, but similar view, of fieldwork within the sciences, see Robert S. Anderson, "The Necessity of Field Methods in the Study of Scientific Research," in *Science and Cultures,* Sociology of the Sciences Yearbook, 1981, ed. Everett Mendelsohn and Yehuda Elkana (Boston: D. Reidel, 1981), 213–44.

CHAPTER 6

1. Kennicott to Baird, 26 Mar. 1863, SIA, RU 7002, Box 27.

2. Ibid., 28 Mar. 1863.

3. Hinsley, *Savages and Scientists,* 38.

4. Kennicott to Baird, 26 Mar. 1863, SIA, RU 7002, Box 27.

5. Baird's Journal, 5 Apr. 1863, SIA, RU 7002, Box 43.

6. Dall, *Baird,* 230–34. See also correspondence between Mary H. Baird and W. H. Dall, SIA, RU 7073, Box 7.

7. Deiss, "Baird and His Collectors," 635–45, describes Baird's reward system.

8. W. O. Hagstrom, *The Scientific Community* (New York: Basic Books, 1965), 12–43, describes the types of rewards and forms of social control that the scientific community uses to nurture its members.

9. One of the few examinations of promotion patterns can be found in J. S. H. Brown, *Strangers in Blood: Fur Trade Company Families in Indian Country* (Vancouver: University of British Columbia Press, 1980), 114, 119, 195–96, 200. See also Judd, "Employment Opportunities for Mixed Bloods." A more comprehensive picture of promotion patterns can be gained through an examination of the careers of the three dozen HBC men found in the *Dictionary of Canadian Biography.* The biographies, listed below, also provide evidence of the discontent that existed because of the company's promotion record. Alice M. Johnson, "Thomas Bird," 2:65; E. E. Rich, "James Isham," 3:301; A. M. Johnson, "Richard Norton," 3:489–90; Irene M. Spry, "Matthew Cocking," 4:156–58; C. S. MacKinnon, "Samuel Hearne," 4:339–42; S. Van Kirk, "Joseph Isbister," 4:380–81; F. Pannekoek, "Humphrey Marten," 4:517–19; S. Van Kirk, "Moses Norton," 4:583–85; Shirlee Anne Smith, "Joseph Colen," 5:194–95; J. S. H. Brown, "Charles T. Isham," 5:450–51; Robert S. Allen, "Peter Fidler," 6:249–52; S. Van Kirk, "John Ballenden," 8:59–60; John E. Foster, "James Bird," 8:90–91; H. Christoph Wolfart, "Joseph Howse," 8:411–14; J. S. H. Brown, "George Keith," 8:453–54; Philip Goldring, "James Keith," 8:454–55; S. Van Kirk, "Donald McKenzie," 8:557–58; Elizabeth Arthur, "Roderick McKenzie," 8:562–63; W. Kaye Lamb, "John McLoughlin," 8:575–81; S. Van Kirk and J. S. H. Brown, "George Nelson," 8:652–53; F. Pannekoek, "Alexander Ross," 8:765–68; C. S. MacKinnon, "James Anderson," 9:5–6; Joan Craig, "John Bell," 9:42–43; J. Craig, "James Robert Clare," 9:130–31; William R. Sampson, "Peter Warren Dease," 9:196–99; W. L. Morton, "George Gladman," 9:319–20; S. Van Kirk, "James Hargrave," 9:364–66; N. Jaye Goossen, "William Mactavish," 9:530–31; W. H. Brooks, "John Peter Pruden," 9:648–49; Hartwell Bowsfield, "Alexander Christie," 10:167–68; W. K. Lamb, "Alexander Caulfield Anderson," 11:16–18; J. E. Rea, "Andrew G. Ballenden Bannatyne," 11:44–47; S. A. Smith, "Richard Hardisty," 11:383–84; S. Van Kirk; "A. K. Isbister," 11:445–46; Edward Charles Shaw, "William Kennedy," 11:470–71; Barry Hyman, "Andrew McDermot," 11:545–46; Garron Wells, "John McLean," 11:569–70; Madge Wolfenden, "John Tod," 11:881–83; W. K. Lamb, "William Fraser Tolmie," 11:885–88.

10. Ross to Baird, 18 Mar. 1861, SIA, HBC Corr. Coll., Folder 36.

11. Ross to Simpson, 14 Dec. 1857, HBCA, PAM, D.5/45, fos. 460–63.

12. Ibid., 3 May 1858, D.5/46, fo. 499.

13. Donald Ross to J. Hargrave, 21 Dec. 1843, National Archives of Canada, MG 19, A 21.

14. B. R. Ross to Baird, 25 Mar. 1860, SIA, HBC Corr. Coll., Folder 36.

15. Baird to Kennicott, 13 Apr. 1861, SIA, RU 7002, Box 3, vol. 5.

16. Mactavish to Baird, 11 Feb. 1867, SIA, HBC Corr. Coll., Folder 33.

17. Ibid., 23 May 1867.

18. "Invoice of Books Etc. Transmitted by the Smithsonian Institution to St. Paul in March 1861 for Bernard Rogan Ross," SIA, RU 7002, Box 66.

19. Ibid.; "Invoice of Boxes Transmitted by the Smithsonian Institution, 1861"; "Lists of Articles Sent from Washington, 14 April 1862," SIA, RU 7002, Box 66.

20. "Lists of Articles"; "Invoice of Boxes."

21. Soon after Kennicott arrived at Norway House, he ordered all of these items. Kennicott to Baird, 18 June 1859, SIA, RU 7215, Box 13.

22. MacFarlane to Kennicott, 9 Sept. 1864; MacFarlane to Baird, 10 May 1864, SIA, RU 7215, Box 14.

23. In 1868 Henry credited MacFarlane with donating more than 10,000 specimens. That estimate probably accounts for the large number of oological specimens that were submitted but not recorded in the HBC collectors' specimen lists. SIAR 1868, 22.

24. MacFarlane to Baird, 10 May 1864, SIA, RU 7215, Box 14.

25. Ibid., 8 Feb., 15 May 1865, 18 May 1866.

26. See correspondence between C. D. Walcott and H. J. Macdonald, 17 June 1918, specifically and between MacFarlane and Walcott and between MacFarlane and Assistant Secretary R. Rathburn generally, U.S. National Museum, Permanent Administrative Files, 1877–1975, SIA, RU 192, Box 37, Folder 4, File #108001/2.

27. Onion to Kennicott, 28 Nov. 1864, SIA, HBC Corr. Coll., Folder 34; MacFarlane to Kennicott, 9 Sept. 1864, SIA, RU 7215, Box 14; Lockhart to Kennicott, 26 June 1865, SIA, HBC Corr. Coll., Folder 24.

28. Kennicott to MacFarlane, 15 Apr. 1864, SIA, RU 7215, Box 13.

29. MacFarlane to Kennicott, 9 Sept. 1864, SIA, RU 7215, Box 14.

30. R. R. MacFarlane, "Notes on the Mammals and Birds of Northern Canada," in Charles Mair, *Through the Mackenzie Basin: A Narrative of the Athabasca and Peace River Treaty Expedition of 1899* (Toronto: Briggs, 1908).

31. MacFarlane's articles on mammals and birds were reprinted. All references are given here. "On an Expedition down the Begh-ula or Anderson River," *Canadian Record of Science* 4 (Jan. 1890): 28–53; "Land and Sea Birds Nesting within the Arctic Circle in the Lower Mackenzie District," *Papers Read before the Historical and Scientific Society of Manitoba (Transactions)* 39 (1890); "Notes on and List of Birds and Eggs collected in Arctic America, 1861–1866" [reprint of "Land and Sea Birds"], *Proceedings of the United States National Museum* 14 (1891): 413–66; "Notes on Mammals Collected and Observed in the Northern Mackenzie River District, North-West Territories of Canada, with Remarks on Explorers and Explorations of the Far North," *Proceedings of the United States National Museum* 28 (1905): 673–764.

32. Ross to Baird, 20 June 1860, SIA, HBC Corr. Coll., Folder 36.

33. Ibid., 18 Mar. 1861.

34. "On the Mammals, Birds &c. of the Mackenzie River District," *Natural History Review*, no. 7 (July 1862), 269–89. The *Canadian Naturalist and Geologist* articles are as follows: "On the Indian Tribes of McKenzie River District and the Arctic Coast," vol. 4 (1859): 190–95; "A Popular Treatise on the Fur-bearing Animals of the Mackenzie River District," vol. 6 (1861): 5–36; "An Account of the Animals Useful in an Economic Point of View to the Various Chipewyan Tribes," vol. 6, 433–41; "List of Species of Mammals and Birds—Collected in McKenzie's River District during 1860–1861," vol. 6, 441–44; "An Account of the Botanical and Mineral Products, Useful to the Chipewyan Tribes of Indians, Inhabiting the Mackenzie River District," vol. 7 (1862): 133–37; "List of Mammals, Birds, and Eggs, Observed in the McKenzie's River District, with Notices," vol. 7, 137–55.

35. Donald Gunn, "Indian Remains near Red River Settlement, Hudson's Bay Territories," SIAR 1867, 399–400, and "An Egging Exploration to Shoal Lake," SIAR 1867, 427–32; S. Jones, "Kutchin (Indian) Tribes," 320–27; W. L. Hardisty, "The Loucheux Indians," SIAR 1866, 311–20; James Lockhart, "Notes on the Habits of the Moose in the Far North of British America in 1865," *Proceedings of the United States National Museum* 13 (1890): 305–8.

36. Evidence of Barnston's sympathies is found in letters to Baird in which Barnston discusses his British, particularly Scottish, and Canadian sympathies. See especially a letter dated 26 Jan. 1860 and an undated letter fragment written in 1859–60, SIA, HBC Corr. Coll., Folders 2 and 3, in which Barnston stated his hopes that the British government would find the money to print the data accumulated by Captain Palliser while in the Northwest. Barnston hoped that the British government would view the data as having "National Interests" rather than as being simply the observations of a "hobbyist." Barnston felt obliged to support McGill College and the Natural History Society of Montreal over the Smithsonian, because the American institution had specimens to "superfuity" [*sic*]. See Barnston to Baird, 20 July 1861, SIA, HBC Corr. Coll., Folder 2.

37. Zeller, *Inventing Canada*, 221.

38. George Barnston's articles in *Canadian Naturalist and Geologist* (or *Canadian Naturalist and Quarterly Journal*, as it was called after 1869) are as follows: "Remarks upon the Geographical Distribution of the Order *Ranunculaceae*, throughout the British Possessions of North America," vol. 2 (1857): 12–20; "Remarks on the Geographical Distribution of Plants in the British Possessions of North America," vol. 3 (1858): 26–32; "Remarks on the Geographical Distribution of the *Cruciferae*, throughout the British Possessions in North America," vol. 4 (1859): 1–12; "Geographical Distribution of the Genus *Allium* in British North America," vol. 4 (1859): 116–21; "Abridged Sketch of the Life of Mr. David Douglas, Botanist, with a Few Details of His Travels and Discoveries," vol. 5 (1860): 120–32, 267–78; "Recollections of the Swans and Geese of Hudson's Bay," vol. 6 (1861): 337–44; "Remarks on the Genus *Lutra*, and on the Species Inhabiting North America," vol. 8 (1863): 147–60; "On a Collection of Plants from British Columbia made by Mr. James Richardson, in the Summer of 1874,"

vol. 8 (1875): 90–94. For a synopsis of Barnston's more important publications, particularly the reference to his article in *Ibis,* see Brown and Van Kirk, "George Barnston," 53.

39. Lindsay, "HBC-Smithsonian Connection," 609.

40. Ross to Baird, 1 June 1862, SIA, HBC Corr. Coll., Folder 36.

41. MacFarlane, "Retired Chief Factor," 7.

42. W. O. Hagstrom, "Gift-giving as an Organizing Principle in Science," in *Sociology of Science: Selected Readings,* ed. Barry Barnes (New York: Penguin Books, 1972), 105–20; Hagstrom, *Scientific Community.*

43. In an analysis of the American scientific community, as exemplified by the American Association for the Advancement of Science, Kohlstedt, *Formation of the American Scientific Community,* 232, shows that only 6 percent of the total population participated actively in scientific activities at midcentury.

44. Ross to Baird, 10 July 1861, SIA, HBC Corr. Coll., Folder 36.

45. Lockhart to Baird, 17 Dec. 1866, 5 Feb., 19 Feb. (telegram), 3 Apr. 1867; Jones to Baird, 7 Nov., 1 Dec. 1866, 15 Apr. 1867, SIA, HBC Corr. Coll., Folders 24, 26.

46. Jones to Baird, 23 Apr. 1867, SIA, HBC Corr. Coll., Folder 24.

47. Deiss, "Baird and His Collectors," 638–39.

48. Baird, Brewer, and Ridgway, *Water Birds of North America,* 445.

49. The common name is referred to in Baird, Brewer, and Ridgway, *History of North American Birds,* 115. The scientific name can be found in Roger Tory Peterson, *A Field Guide to Western Birds,* 2d ed. (Boston: Houghton Mifflin, 1961); it is, however, difficult to determine whether Baird or some more recent ornithologist bestowed this honor on MacFarlane.

50. Fielding B. Meek, "Remarks on the Geology of the Mackenzie River, with Figures and Descriptions of Fossils from That Region, in the Museum of the Smithsonian Institution, Chiefly Collected by the Late Robert Kennicott," *Transactions of the Chicago Academy of Sciences* 1 (1867–69): 83, 88–89.

51. The classic study of the sociology of science is Robert K. Merton, *Science, Technology, and Society in Seventeenth-Century England,* Osiris: Studies on the History and Philosophy of Science (Bruges, Belgium: St. Catherine's Press, 1938; reprint, New York: Howard Fertig, 1970, with new preface), but Merton followed that pioneering work with several other sociological studies. See especially his *Social Theory and Social Structure* (1949, 1957; reprint, New York: Free Press, 1968) and "The Sociology of Science: An Episodic Memoir," in *The Sociology of Science in Europe,* ed. R. K. Merton and Jerry Gaston (Carbondale: Southern Illinois University Press, 1977), 3–141. See also Bernard Barber, *Science and the Social Order* (New York: Free Press, 1952, 1962; reprint, Westport, Conn.: Greenwood Press, 1978); J. Ben-David, *The Scientist's Role in Society* (Englewood Cliffs, N.J.: Prentice-Hall, 1971); Barnes, ed., *Sociology of Science;* and E. Mendelsohn, introduction to *Science and Cultures,* ed. Mendelsohn and Elkana, vii–xiii. For more-specific discussions on status and role in the scientific community, see Hagstrom, *Scientific Community* and "Gift-giving," and Jerry Gaston, *The Reward System in British and American Science* (Toronto: John Wiley and Sons, 1978).

CHAPTER 7

1. Memorandum in Dall Diaries, 1 Feb. 1865, SIA, RU 7073, Box 20. Dall, *Baird*, 367–71, 377, also contains some important documents pertaining to the early organization of the scientific corps. Rosemary Neering, *Continental Dash: The Russian-American Telegraph* (Ganges, B.C.: Horsdal and Schubart, 1989), provides a lively narrative of the progress of the expedition, with a special emphasis on commercial factors. For a good discussion of the contributions of and difficulties encountered by the scientific corps of the Western Union expedition, see Morgan B. Sherwood, *Exploration of Alaska, 1865–1900* (New Haven, Conn.: Yale University Press, 1965), 15–35.

2. Cutting to Baird, 8 Nov. 1864, in Dall, *Baird*, 371.

3. Ibid., 1, 24 Aug., 24 Oct., 8 Nov. 1864, 367–71.

4. Ibid., 1 Aug., 8 Nov. 1864, 369.

5. Ibid.

6. Neering, *Continental Dash*, 39. On the construction of the British Columbia portion of the line, see pp. 37–62.

7. See correspondence between Baird and Kennicott during 1863, 1864, and the beginning of 1865, SIA, RU 7002, Box 27.

8. Kennicott to Baird, 17 Jan. 1865, SIA, RU 7002, Box 27. See also Kennicott to MacFarlane, 15 Apr. 1864, in Dall, *Baird*, 372–77.

9. Kennicott to Baird, 24 Jan. 1865, SIA, RU 7002, Box 27.

10. Cutting to Baird, 24 Oct. 1864, in Dall, *Baird*, 370–71.

11. Kennicott to Baird, 7 Jan. 1865, SIA, RU 7002, Box 27; list of Kennicott's telegrams, Apr. 1865, SIA, RU 7213, Box 1; memoranda in Dall Diaries, 1 Feb. 1865, SIA, RU 7073, Box 20.

12. Dall Diaries, 4 May–10 July 1865, SIA, RU 7073, Box 20.

13. Kennicott to Baird, 9 July 1865, SIA, RU 7213, Box 1.

14. Ibid., 2, 3 June, 9, 23, 28 July, 9, 16 Sept. 1865; Dall to Baird, 16 Aug. 1865, SIA, RU 7213, Box 1.

15. On Hyde and intrigues in San Francisco, see Dall to Baird, 19 Sept. 1865, SIA, RU 7073, Box 2.

16. Kennicott to Baird, 3 June 1865, SIA, RU 7213, Box 1.

17. Ibid., 9 July 1865.

18. Dall Diaries, 7 July 1865, SIA, RU 7073, Box 20.

19. Dall to Baird, 4 Oct. 1865, SIA, RU 7213, Box 1.

20. "Journal of William Ennis," *California Historical Quarterly* 33 (1954): 4. For information on Ennis and other men recruited in San Francisco for Kennicott's expedition, see also Dall to Baird, 26 Apr. 1867, SIA, RU 7002, Box 18.

21. Bulkley's orders to Kennicott, 8 Sept. 1865, SIA, RU 7213, Box 1.

22. Kennicott to Baird, 23 July 1865, SIA, RU 7213, Box 1.

23. Ibid., 9 July 1865. On Bischoff, see also Sherwood, *Exploration of Alaska*, 23–24. For details of his collections, see "Catalogues of Specimens Taken on Expeditions, 1865–1880," SIA, RU 7073, Box 26.

24. Dall to Baird, 10 Nov. 1865, SIA, RU 7213, Box 1. See also "Catalogues of Specimens."

25. Events of September 1865 to May 1866 are described in George Adams's Diary, BCA, J I W 52.

26. Dall to Baird, 4 Oct. 1865, SIA, RU 7213, Box 1.

27. Kennicott to Baird, 23 July, 16 Sept. 1865, SIA, RU 7213, Box 1; Dall to Baird, 26 Apr. 1867, SIA, RU 7002, Box 18.

28. Kennicott to Baird, 23 July 1865, SIA, RU 7213, Box 1. Dall noted Bulkley's parsimony in provisioning Kennicott's expedition: "In 1866 for *40 men, 6000 lbs of flour* were left, while 8000 lbs had hardly proved sufficient for the party of 1865 consisting of 15 men" (Dall to Baird, 26 Apr. 1867, SIA, RU 7002, Box 18). George Adams also commented frequently on the sorry state of their provisions, as in this example:

> [T]he living is pretty rough, bean soup twice a day, very little bread, *very* weak tea, ham occasionally, canned beef "simmi occasionally" our Molasses, Sugar, Coffee, canned vegetables, Apple Sauce (dried apples dissicated potatoes has vanished like a beautiful dream, and we must "live close" on our Flour, Hard Tack, Bacon, and tea.) These will soon run out, certainly no body of men could have more reason to upbraid a Company than we have. Left in a country like this where a person requires twice as much food, as in any other; with hardly half Army Rations is very rough to say the least. (Adams Diary, 12 Jan. 1866, BCA, J I W 52)

29. Adams Diary, 20 Oct. 1865, BCA, J I W 52.

30. Numerous references to the lack of game are found in the diaries of George Adams and Fred Smith, BCA, J I W 52.

31. Kennicott to Baird, 3 June, 9 Sept. 1865, SIA, RU 7213, Box 1.

32. Adams Diary, 7 Nov. 1865, BCA, J I W 52.

33. Ibid.

34. See SIAR 1865, 61–62, 86–87; and Kennicott to Baird, 3 Apr. 1865, SIA, RU 7213, Box 1.

35. Kennicott to Baird, 23 July, 16 Sept. 1865, SIA, RU 7213, Box 1.

36. Several authors have implied that Kennicott was unstable. See Zochert, "Notes on a Young Naturalist," 34–47; William Fitzhugh, "The Smithsonian's Alaska Connection: Nineteenth-Century Explorers and Anthropologists," *Alaska Journal* 11 (1981): 194; Sherwood, *Exploration of Alaska,* 19; and Neering, *Continental Dash,* 170–75.

37. Kennicott to Baird, 20 Oct. 1863, SIA, RU 7002, Box 27. See also letters of 17 Aug. and 24 Sept. 1863 for similar passages.

38. See correspondence between Kennicott and Baird, SIA, RU 7002, Box 27.

39. Kennicott to Baird, 23 June 1861, SIA, RU 7215, Box 13.

40. Ibid., 21 Jan. 1862.

41. See letters to Baird. Kennicott also described the state of his health to Baird's daughter, Lucy, and more-oblique references to his physical condition can be found in his "Rubbaboo Journal." See letters in Robert Kennicott Papers, SIA, RU 7215, Box 13; letters to Lucy Hunter Baird in Spencer Fullerton Baird Papers, SIA, RU 7002, Box 37; and Kennicott's journal, edited by J. A. James, in *The First Scientific Exploration of Russian America.*

42. See diaries of William Dall, George Adams, Fred Smith, and William Ennis. See also Dall to Baird, 26 Apr. 1867, SIA, RU 7002, Box 18.

43. There are two fairly detailed (and somewhat romanticized) accounts of Kennicott's last night. Dall wrote:

He sat up late and wrote. He then lay down on the broad shelf which served for a common bed for six, where Pease and Ketchum were lying. He lay for a short time and Ketchum who was in a half dozy, half awake state; felt him reach up to his fire bag in which his revolver was put, hanging above his (Ks) head. K woke up presently and saw his revolver missing. He inquired for it and the Major handed it back to him. He then went to sleep again while Kennicott took up his hat and walked out; this was about two or three oclock A.M. K. heard him walking outside in the yard until he fell asleep. Breakfast being ready, he was not forthcoming and Ketchum immediately felt that something was wrong. Lunchy and Ive two Mahlemuts were sent out to call him but did not see him. Ketchum immediately dispatched Mike Lebarge and Pease down the beach and Smith and Adams up, and the two former soon came upon him lying as if asleep on the beach about 300 yards south of the fort. His compass was open by his side, lines indicating the bearings of various points were traced in the gravel; he lay stretched at full length, straight, on his back with his arms folded on his breast, and his felt hat had fallen back, just off his forehead. The body was already "in rigor mortis." (Dall to Baird, 26 Apr. 1867, SIA, RU 7002, Box 18)

Kennicott's friends wrote another rendition in *Transactions of the Chicago Academy of Sciences:*

He rose (it was the season of nights only an hour or two long) and drew up directions (*"in case of any accident happening to me"*) for the carrying on of the explorations, under the superintendence of his faithful companion, Ketchum; and wrote a note to the Engineer in Chief of the expedition, briefly recounting the obstacles he had met with, and saying, what no one who knew him ever doubted, that he had done his best to carry out the objects of the expedition. This was between four and five in the morning. The sun was shining brightly out of doors; and much relieved by having thus provided for any emergency which might come to pass, he asked Ketchum, who was half dozing on the bed, to come out and walk with him. Ketchum excused himself, as he had hardly rested from the hard work of the previous day. The Major stepped out, and for a few moments Ketchum heard him walking up and down in the yard outside, humming a lively *voyageur's* song. Tarentof afterward related, with tears in his eyes, how, passing out of the stockade to the beach in front of the fort, where the ice-laden waters were hurrying toward the sea, the Major had nodded a good-morning, and used the Russian salutation (*s'dras-dui*), the last word he spoke to any one in life.

About eight o'clock breakfast was put on the table, but no one knew where the Major was. After some delay, as he did not come, they sat down, but every one felt anxious, as he was usually most punctual at the table. Directly after breakfast all dispersed in search of him, but he was not to be found. All were now seriously alarmed, and went out again for a more careful and extended search, taking all the Indian and Eskimo servants with them.

Mike Lebarge and an Eskimo lad named Lunchy went south from the fort toward the Nulato River, along the soft muddy beach. A dark object, a few hundred yards from the fort, caught Mike's eye. On approaching, their worst fears were more than realized. On the beach was placed the Major's pocket compass, and lines indicating the bearings of the various mountains in sight, drawn in the soft alluvium, showing that he had been busy in adding to his material for a map of the country around Nulato when death took him. His remains lay as he had fallen; not a motion or a struggle after he fell. His death had been quick and painless, as his life had been noble and generous. He lay upon his back, his arms across his breast; his hat, a black felt broad-brim, just touched his forehead with one edge, so that hardly a breath was needed to displace it. His eyes were half closed, his face calm and peaceful. ("Biography of Robert Kennicott," 223)

44. George Adams, *Life in the Yukon, 1865–1867*, ed. R. A. Pierce (Kingston, Ont.: Limestone Press, 1982), is quoted in Neering, *Continental Dash*, 174.

45. The symptoms of strychnine poisoning begin 15 to 30 minutes after ingestion of the poison and include hyperreflexia, muscular stiffness, and generalized convulsions that are characterized by hyperextension, with the arms being flexed over the chest or rigidly extended. Strychnine poisoning produces death from respiratory failure within one to three hours. Most disturbing is that the victim remains conscious during the painful convulsions and is apprehensive and fearful throughout the illness. See M. N. Gleason, R. E. Gosselin, H. C. Hodge, and R. P. Smith, *Clinical Toxicology of Commercial Product, Acute Poisoning*, 3d ed. (Baltimore: Williams and Wilkins, 1969), 214–16.

46. Cyril John Polson and D. J. Gee, *The Essentials of Forensic Medicine*, 3d ed. (Oxford: Pergamon Press, 1973), 18–22. For information on strychnine and "instant rigor mortis," see p. 22.

47. Dall to Lizzie Merriam, 29 Sept. 1866, SIA, RU 7073, Box 2, cited in Sherwood, *Exploration of Alaska*, 24.

CONCLUSION

1. The functionalism of science is discussed in Robert M. Young, "Science as Culture," *Quarto* 2 (1979): 7–8, and "Science Is a Labour Process," *Science for People* 43–44 (1979): 31–37.

2. See especially James, *First Scientific Exploration*. See also Archibald W. Shiels, *Seward's Icebox: A Few Notes on the Development of Alaska, 1867–1932* (Bellingham, Wash.: Union Printing Co., 1933); Charles Vevier, "The Collins Overland Line and American Continentalism," *Pacific Historical Review* 28, no. 3 (1959); Fitzhugh, "Smithsonian's Alaska Connection"; and Neering, *Continental Dash*.

3. Sherwood, *Exploration of Alaska*, is the most notable proponent of this view, but see also Ronald J. Jensen, *The Alaska Purchase and Russian-American Relations* (Seattle: University of Washington Press, 1975). An examination of the Smithsonian records supports their stance.

4. See especially Kennicott's report to William Ennis, 18 Mar. 1866, SIA, RU 7073, Box 18.

5. Kennicott to MacFarlane, 15 Apr. 1864, in Dall, *Baird,* 372–77.

6. Sumner's speech is reprinted in Shiels, *Seward's Icebox,* 185–297.

7. Richard Ruggles, *A Country So Interesting: The Hudson's Bay Company and Two Centuries of Mapping, 1670–1870* (Kingston and Montreal: McGill-Queen's University Press, 1991), 110–19. See also Valerian Lada-Mocarski, *Bibliography of Books on Alaska Published before 1868* (New Haven, Conn.: Yale University Press, 1969), and Wickersham, *Bibliography of Alaskan Literature.*

8. Dall to Baird, 27 Sept. 1866, SIA, RU 7213, Box 1; SIAR 1868, 23.

9. SIAR 1867, 73; "Catalogues of Specimens Taken on Expeditions, 1865–1880"; Sherwood, *Exploration of Alaska,* 39.

10. In "The Yukon River Region, Alaska," *Journal of the American Geographical Society of New York* 3 (1873): 158–92, Captain Charles Raymond of the U.S. Corps of Topographical Engineers discounted assertions about the agricultural, mining, and lumbering potential of Alaska as overstated and belonging to the "category of things that are probable . . . [and] destined to develop slowly." He pointed out that the value of the inland fur trade had been "greatly exaggerated" and that the only dependable and valuable natural resource was fish.

11. Although I was unable to uncover any documentary evidence in Baird's correspondence with Sumner and Seward that Smithsonian data were traded for increased government appropriations, there was a substantial increase in congressional funding to Baird's department coincidental with the debates over the purchase of Alaska. Until 1867 the Smithsonian Institution never received more than $4,000 per year for the care of government collections. In 1867 Baird received $10,000 for that purpose. The 1868 and 1869 appropriations returned to the previous level, but in 1870 the $10,000 grant was reinstated. The grant increased to $15,000 in 1872, and it continued to increase after the Smithsonian was designated as the National Museum. See "Congressional Appropriations for Care of Government Collections," reprinted in William J. Rhees, ed., *The Smithsonian Institution: Documents Relative to Its Origin and History, 1835–1899,* Smithsonian Misc. Coll., vol. 42 (1900), 607–783.

APPENDIX

1. SIAR 1862, 56; 1865, 85. See also SIA, Accession Records, U.S. National Museum, RU 699T, or on microfilm (RU 305).

2. Accession Records, U.S. National Museum.

3. Only one specimen was entered in the accession books in 1870, but it was credited to B. R. Ross. The specimen was donated by Mrs. Baird in Ross's name because he had sent her a present of native handiwork some years earlier. See Registers, Accession Records, Department of Anthropology, NMNH, vols. 1–3, SIA, RU 6990T. MacFarlane sent specimens to the Smithsonian after 1871, but there was a period of almost 20 years in which he sent no specimens. He sent

approximately 400 specimens between 1889 and 1892 when he was chief factor in charge of the Cumberland District in the lower Saskatchewan. See U.S. National Museum, Permanent Administrative Files, 1877–1975, SIA, RU 192, Folder 4, Box 37, File #108001/2.

4. For the sources of the information in the table, see note 29 for Chapter 1.

INDEX